CRICUT DESIGN SPACE

A COMPLETE AND PRACTICAL BEGINNERS GUIDE TO CRICUT DESIGN SPACE

AUTHOR

Jane Jones

© Copyright 2019 by Jane Jones

All Rights Reserved.

This document is geared towards providing exact and reliable information in regards to the topic and issue covered. The publication is sold with the idea that the publisher is not required to render accounting, officially permitted, or otherwise, qualified services. If advice is necessary, legal or professional, a practiced individual in the profession should be ordered.

From a Declaration of Principles which was accepted and approved by a Committee of the American Bar Association and a Committee of Publishers and Associations.

In no way is it legal to reproduce, duplicate, or transmit any part of this document in either electronic means or in printed format. Fileing of this publication is strictly prohibited and any storage of this document is not allowed unless with written permission from the publisher. All rights reserved.

The information provided herein is stated to be truthful and consistent, in that any liability, in terms of inattention or otherwise, by any usage or abuse of any policies, processes, or directions contained within is the solitary and utter responsibility of the recipient reader. Under no circumstances will any legal responsibility or blame be held against the publisher for any reparation, damages, or monetary loss due to the information herein, either directly or indirectly.

Respective authors own all copyrights not held by the publisher.

The information herein is offered for informational purposes solely, and is universal as so. The presentation of the information is without contract or any type of guarantee assurance.

The trademarks that are used are without any consent, and the publication of the trademark is without permission or backing by the trademark owner. All trademarks and brands within this book are for clarifying purposes only and are owned by the owners themselves, not affiliated with this document.

Table Of Texts

Table Of Texts 3

Chapter One: Cricut Vocabulary 4

Cricus Cheat Sheet 17

Chapter Two: How To Use A PDF File In Cricut Design Space Using Different Devices 21

Chapter Three: How To Work With Images And Edit Panel 24

Images 24

Edit Panel, Fonts and Images 62

Chapter Four: Apparatus 67

Chapter Five: Working With Multiple Lines of text 71

Text Edit Panel 71

Chapter One: Cricut Vocabulary

The whole of the terms I've remembered for this jargon is a piece of the equipment (Cricut machine and frill) and furthermore programming instruments and settings that are significant during the designing and cutting procedure.

They are to request

Adaptative System

The innovation controls the Cricut Maker and permits it to cut with 10X the quality that any of the Explore family machines.

Attach

It's a setting that permits you to allocate a Layer to another.

For example, if you are making a card and need to add text to it, you have to advise your Cricut where to write. By choosing the two things (the map, and message) and attaching them, your Cricut will now where to write.

You can likewise utilize "Connect" with score lines and images that are in various layers; however, you need them to remain together when you send your task to cut.

Sponsorship

Sponsorship is a material that is reinforced with a surface so it very well may be cut appropriately.

Materials, for example, vinyl, Infusible Ink move sheets, and reinforced texture (to use with fortified texture cutting edge) are required to have support.

Sharp edge

Sharp edges are the instruments that permit you to cut your materials. You will require a choice cutting edge contingent upon the machine and the thickness of your stuff.

Edge, Fine Point

The Fine Point edge is the most well-known, and it accompanies the whole of the Cricut Machines; this cutting edge is ideal for making perplexing cuts, and 'it's intended to cut medium-weight materials.

Sharp edge, Deep Point

If you have to cut thicker materials, the Deep Point Blade will be your closest companion. You can utilize it with any of the Cricut Explore Family machines or Cricut Maker!

The edge of this edge is so a lot more extreme (60 degrees contrasted with 45 degrees for the fine point edge) This permits the Blade to enter and cut unpredictable cuts in thick materials.

Sharp edge, Bonded Fabric

The Bonded Fabric Blade was expressly intended to cut texture (don't utilize it for whatever else). The texture you are going to slice should be clung to a sponsorship material.

Sharp edge, Knife Blade

The blade sharp edge is intended to slice through thick materials, for example, balsa wood, mat panel, chip panel, and so on.

It must be utilized with the Cricut Maker.

Sharp edge, Rotary

The Rotary Blade slices through, practically, and texture. What's more, the best part is that you 'needn't bother with any sponsorship material to balance out the texture on the mat.

It must be utilized with the Cricut Maker.

Brayer

A tool that permits you to tie down your material to the mat.

It's, for the most part, used to adhere texture to the "Pink Mat,"

Bright Pad

It's an extra that will light up the surface that you are taking a shot at.

The Bright pad is a wise project if you have to weed enormous and mind-boggling designs (particularly around evening time). It likewise works superbly when following images and gems making

Shape

Shape, in Cricut Design Space, is an instrument that permits you to delete/conceal undesirable pieces from your projects; this choice is incredibly ground-breaking since you can adjust your tasks to make an entire distinctive impact or feel.

Cricut Access

Cricut Access is a paid participation that gives you moment access to an astounding and monster library loaded up with over 90.000 images, many text styles, and prepared to cut tasks.

Contingent upon the arrangement you have, you can get different advantages like limits on authorized images, text styles, and physical items.

Not to be mistaken for Cricut Design Space.

Cricut Design Space

Cricut Design Space is the place the whole of the enchantment occurs before you cut your activities. From this space, you will do the whole of the editings, for example, including font styles, images evolving hues, and so on.

If you need to get the best use out of your Cricut, you have to learn and ace Design Space.

I realize it appears to be overpowering from the outset, yet once you make a plunge, nothing will stop you!

Cricut's product it's free, and you can utilize it with your machine whenever you need it. Try not to mistake it for Cricut Access.

Cricut Explore Family Machines

The whole of the Cricut Explore Family machines can cut similar materials, and utilize similar devices. Notwithstanding, every single one of them has various highlights.

Cricut Explore, One

Firstborn of the Explore family and just has one device holder, so you cut and draw, score independently. You have to interface it with a link to your PC or purchase a different connector.

Cricut Explore, Air

The Explore Air has Bluetooth and both tool holders so you can cut and draw simultaneously.

Cricut Explore, Air 2

Has similar abilities, that the Explore Air, however, 'it's multiple times quicker.

Cricut Maker

The Maker is the freshest machine; not at all like any of the Explore family machines, the cutting power of the Cricut Maker is 10X more grounded; this quality is the thing that permits it to cut thick materials, for example, calfskin, balsa wood, chip panel, mat panel, and so forth.

Cricut Pens

Any of the Cricut Machines will permit you to write and draw on your materials. Pens are perfect for scrapbooking, card making, color pages, and so on.

The admonition with pens is that you can just utilize Cricut Brand pens; no stresses however, there are innumerable hues and various completions like metallics, sparkle, gel, and so forth.

Note: There are numerous tips and deceives to utilize different pens with your Cricut, however you need a pen connector.

Cuttlebug

The Cuttlebus is a little and manual bite the dust cutting machine that doesn't require any web or power. The Cuttlebug works with plates made out of metal (they arrive in a wide assortment of designs) that can embellish or cut your materials.

If you need to get one of these little machines you better rush in light of the fact that Cricut reported that they wouldn't continue delivering them.

Cut Files

Additionally called SVG, or Vector illustrations are images that you can increment or diminish in size without losing quality. You can transfer your own to Desing Space, or utilize the ones from Cricut Access.

Not at all like PNG or JPG images that are constrained, SVG files permit you to redo the whole of the subtleties (layers) of your designs like color, size, line type, and so forth.

Decal

Decals are designs made out of vinyl (perpetual or removable) that can be moved to various surfaces like mugs, dividers, metal, and so forth.

Easypress

An EasyPress is a gadget that permits you to move your Iron-On or HTV (Heat Transfer Vinyl) designs to surfaces like texture, wood, paper, and so forth.

The manner in which you apply warmth to your Iron-On is basic, in such a case that you 'don't do it the correct way; you will be baffled, yet you will likewise hazard destroying your materials.

Each kind of Iron-On Vinyl and the surface you need to apply it requires various temperatures and a perfect time for appropriate exchange.

The EasyPress permits you to control all factors; in this manner, all re-thinking and questions will be good and gone.

Easypress, Mat

Cricut suggests utilizing an Easypres Mat since it permits you to press the article of clothing further against the warmth. If you 'don't have it, utilize a towel between or underneath your T-shirt. It works similarly also.

If you don't utilize the mat or the towel, you may require more presses to move your design to your surface.

Note: You should utilize the Easypress Mat if utilizing Infusible Ink.

Easypress, Mini

Much the same as its name says it, the Easypress Mini is a minuscule press intended to move Iron-On or Infusible Ink in parts that a customary Easypress can arrive at like shoes, caps, pockets, doll garments, and so on.

It has three diverse temperature settings, and it can warm up to 400 °F.

If you love everything minor, the EP little is an incredible instrument to have.

Flatten

This tool is additional help for the Print then cut setting; when you change the fill from no fill to print, that applies to only one layer. Yet, imagine a scenario in which you wish to do it to various shapes at the time.

When you are finished with your design, select the layers you need to print altogether, and afterward select flatten.

Lodging

Lodging is the thing that holds the sharp edge set up. When your sharp edge is expected for a change, you don't have to change the lodging.

Lodging, Drive

This kind of lodging is explicitly intended for the Cricut Maker just, and they contrast from standard lodging sharp edges since they have a brilliant top tool that is driven by the Adaptive Tool System.

Drive Housing sharp edges accompany a plastic spread that ought to be left consistently to keep the tools clean.

Infusible Ink

Cricut Infusible Ink is a kind of innovation that permits you to make and move your designs to a base material. What makes this innovation so one of a kind is that the Infusible Ink move will get one with the base material you pick.

The outcomes subsequent to applying Cricut Infusible ink are amazing and very high caliber. They are flawlessly smooth, 'don't strip away, and they will remain in your base material until the end of time.

This line of items is very dubious to utilize and before endeavoring to cause anything with them, it would be ideal if you for the good of your pocket, ensure you adhere to all directions to the tee.

Layer

Layers speak to each and every component or design that is on the canvas zone.

Consider it like garments; when you get dressed, you have different layers that make up your outfit; and relying upon the day, or season, your outfit can be straightforward or complex.

Thus, for a freezing day, your layers would be clothing, pants, shirt, coat, sock, boots, gloves, and so forth.; and for a day at the pool, you would just have one layer, a Swim Suit!

The equivalent occurs with a design; contingent upon the multifaceted nature of the task you are taking a shot at, 'you'll have various sorts of layers 'that will make up your whole project.

Linetype and Fill

Linetype will tell your machine when you are cutting your project, what instrument you will utilize. At the present time, there are seven choices (Cut, Draw, Score, Engrave, Deboss, Wave, Perf).

If you have a Cricut Maker, all choices will be accessible, however if you have an Explore you will just have the Cut, Draw, and the Score choice.

The fill choice is for printing and examples.

It might be actuated when you have Cut as a "Linetype." No Fill implies that you 'won't print anything.

Mat

A Cricut Mat is where you cut the whole of your undertakings. At this moment, there are four unique kinds of mats, Light Grip (blue), Standard Grip (green), Strong Grip (purple), and texture (pink).

Mat, Light Grip (blue)

This mat was intended to cut lightweight materials (paper, vinyl, slender cardstock).

Mat, Standard Grip (green)

The Standard Grip Mat is the most widely recognized and moderate one, and 'it's intended to work with medium-weight materials like cardstock, creased paper, sparkle vinyl, and so forth.

Mat, Strong Grip (purple)

This mat was intended to hold set up overwhelming materials like wood, sparkle cardstock, chip panel, and so forth.

Mat, Fabric (pink)

The Fabric Grip mat is explicitly intended to cut texture. Fortified with any of the Cricut investigate Family machines or just all alone with the Rotary cutting edge and the Cricut Maker.

Mirror

Mirroring is the act of flipping an image or design on a flatten design during the cutting procedure; this is basically finished with Iron-On vinyl and Infusible Ink projects.

If you don't mirror your images when working with these sorts of materials, when you move them, they will look in reverse.

Print then Cut

Print then Cut is a choice that permits you to print your designs and afterward cut around them. When you have a component or configuration set to print then cut; Design Space will send it to your home printer, and afterward it will cut it.

Print then Cut is perfect for making stickers, blessing labels, and different kinds of tasks that need various blends of hues and examples.

Pretty Side Down

This term is utilized a great deal by practically all bloggers, and it implies that you have to put your materials (paper, vinyl, and so forth.) with the most brilliant, or lovely side down.

Putting materials quite side down is a typical practice when your tasks expect you to mirror your images, and you are cutting things like Iron-On Vinyl and one side covered materials need to score on.

If you don't set your material "entirely side down" when prescribed, your last project will look in reverse.

Dreadful!

Clicky Swap

It's one of the various lodgings Cricut has for their cutting edges and tips. Starting at now, the QuickSwap framework permits you to utilize five different instruments (2 sharp edges, and three hints)

Quick Swap, Scoring wheel

The Scoring Wheel is an instrument that permits you to make wonderful, restless, and fresh creases on your materials.

Quick Swap, Debossing Tip

This tip will push the material in, and it will make delightful and nitty-gritty designs. The debossing will carry your activities to an unheard-of flatten as a result of the detail you would now be able to add to your designs.

Quick Swap, Engraving Tip

The Engraving Tip permits you to etch a wide assortment of materials. Do you have a pooch? Shouldn't something be said about making a canine tag?

You can make monograms, and other cool designs on aluminum sheets or anodized aluminum to uncover the silver underneath.

Quick Swap, Perforation Blade

This specific cutting edge will permit you to make projects with a tear finish. With this instrument, another universe of conceivable outcomes has open. You can make coupons, wager tickets, and so forth.!

Quick Swap, Wavy Blade

Rather than cutting on straight lines like the rotating or excellent point sharp edge, this instrument will make wavy impacts on your finished products.

Blessing Tags, flags, cards, envelopes, and one of a kind vinyl decals are a portion of the undertakings that will profit by this device.

Prepared to Cut Projects

Prepared to Cut undertakings are as of now designed and accessible to remove right. There are a large number of them, and it's a great path for you to begin with your Cricut.

These undertakings are delightful, and you can discover a project for each home stylistic theme, occasion, unique event, and so on.

Additionally, if you don't care for a portion of the subtleties of the projects, you can likewise adjust them, so they fit the whole of your imaginative needs.

Scrubber

The scrubber is one of the basic Cricut instruments, and if you possess, or are going to purchase a machine, it is an unquestionable requirement to get one.

When you finish a cut, there are a lot of odds and ends that are remaining on your mat. With this device, you can scratch them off rapidly.

Cut

The Slice device is a choice in Cricut Design Space that permits you to part and harvest out two covering images or layers to make a totally different design.

With Slice, you can make excellent cut-out impacts on your activities. The potential outcomes are huge.

Scoring Stylus

The Scoring Stylus is another basic tool that each Cricut proprietor ought to have. Not exclusively it's very reasonable, however it will likewise assist you with creating score lines for a simple overlap.

Not at all like the Scoring Wheel that solitary works with the Cricut Maker, the Stylus works with both the Maker and Explore Machines.

The Stylus is an unquestionable requirement if you need to make boxes, cards, or any task that requires folds.

Move Tape

This tape is utilized to move changeless or removable vinyl decals to your surface. Most regular surfaces are mugs, dividers, vehicles, and windows.

Vinyl

Vinyl is a sort of material that adheres to a wide assortment of surfaces, for example, mugs, texture, windows, wood, metal, and so on.

Not all vinyl materials work the equivalent; contingent upon the undertaking and surface you are working with, you'll have to utilize an choice sort of vinyl.

Working with vinyl has an expectation to absorb information, however once you've done two or three activities with it, you'll review that the guidelines are anything but difficult to follow and you simply expected to rehearse.

Vinyl, Iron-On

Iron-On (additionally called Heat Transfer Vinyl, HTV) is a sort of material that should be warmed to be moved effectively; 'It's utilized to modify T-shirts, wood, metal and even paper!

Sparkle, foil, designed, and holographic vinyl are a portion of the various styles of Iron-On.

Vinyl, Removable

Kind of vinyl that is suggested for indoor use and that can be expelled effortlessly.

Vinyl, Permanent

Kind of vinyl that is suggested for open air utilization since it can withstand high and cold temperatures. Changeless vinyl is perfect for making vehicle decals and finishing open air ceramics.

A few activities that are for "indoor use" however can profit by this tough material are mugs, glasses, and tumblers.

Weeder, Weeding

One of Cricut's generally significant and basic instruments. The weeder has a sharp snare that permits you to expel negative pieces of your design once your machine is finished with the cutting procedure.

The demonstration of evacuating the negative cuts is called weeding, and it's very unwinding!

The weeder is particularly useful when working with vinyl and different activities that have many-sided cuts.

Weld

The Weld Tool in Cricut Design Space permits you to contour numerous layers into a solitary one. This instrument is very convenient as it will empower you to make new designs and components out of straightforward shapes.

Cricus Cheat Sheet

Cricut Design Space Cheat Sheet
by: Lorrie Nunemaker

Slice, Weld, Attach, Flatten & Contour

Slice

1. Slice will cut one image from another (like a cookie cutter)
2. Slice works with two layers only.
3. Select two layers, select Slice, pull layers apart
4. Slice is often used to cut one shape from another
5. Slice is often used to delete a part of an image
6. Slice is often used to create an outline of a font or image

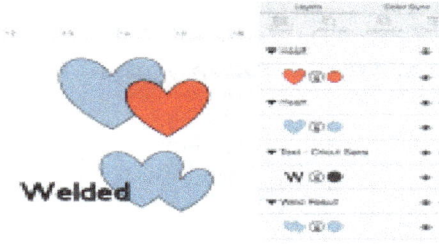

Weld

1. Weld will join two or more layers together
2. Weld will delete cut lines between overlapping objects
3. Weld will create one layer in the same color from two or more layers.
4. Weld is often used to join script text
5. Weld is often used to combine multiple layers into one layer so that they may be sliced

Slice, Flatten, Weld, Contour

Cricut Design Space Cheat Sheet
by: Lorrie Nunemaker

Uploading a PNG or JPG Image

1. Click Upload > Upload Image >
2. Drag and drop or click browse to navigate to your image

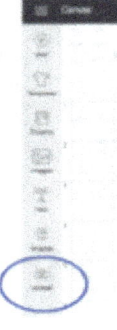  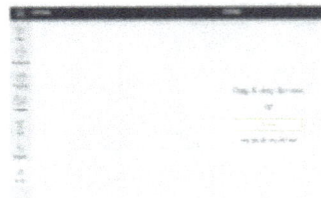

3. Choose Complex to save the most detail (choose simple or moderate to save less detail).

4. Click the preview window to check cut lines. Use select & erase to delete any background you do NOT want to cut. Click continue.

5. Save as a Print then Cut Image
6. Add tags (Key words) to help find the image later
7. Click Save
8. Image will be in the recently uploaded images
9. You can also find the image by clicking Images > Filter > Uploaded > (Enter key words in the search bar)

Cricut Design Space Cheat Sheet
by: Lorrie Nunemaker

Slice, Weld, Attach, Flatten & Contour

Attach

1. Attach will keep the placement of items from the design area to the cutting mat.
2. Select desired object layers and select Attach
3. Attach is often used to hold word art / text in place

Flatten

1. Flatten is used to change multiple layers into one Print then Cut layer
2. Flatten is used to keep printed text on an object such as a card or envelope
3. Flatten is ONLY used when Printing

Contour

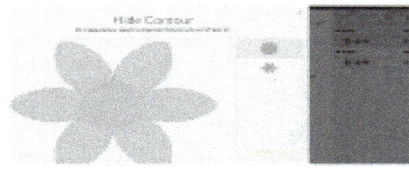

1. Contour is used to delete cut areas from a single layer

Chapter Two: How To Use A PDF File In Cricut Design Space Using Different Devices

To begin with, you should realize that you can't transfer a PDF file to Cricut® Design Space. For ideal outcomes, you should choose a PNG document at whatever point conceivable. Other basic document types that you can transfer incorporate .jpg, .bmp and .gif image files. You can likewise transfer vector images including .svg and .dxf documents.

Not all is awful news however with regards to PDF archives. In spite of the fact that you can't transfer them straightforwardly to Cricut® Design Space, you can change over them to PNG organization and afterward transfer them. All in all, how would you convert a PDF to PNG? It's a lot simpler than you may have ever envisioned!

The most effective method to EASILY CONVERT A PDF TO PNG FORMAT

In all honesty, there is a free online tool that will rapidly and effectively help you to change over your PDF reports to PNG position in merely seconds!

- After you have downloaded the PDF file to your PC, open your program and go to png2pdf.com.
- Click the Upload Files
- This will dispatch the Open document exchange box. Find the PDF you might want to change over (likely in your Downloads envelope), selectthe PDF document and select
- The file will be transferred. You should review an improvement pointer and once the file has been transferred and changed over, you'll review a Download button beneath the little image of the transferred document. Selectthe Download

- The document will be downloaded as a ZIP file and show up in the status bar close to the base of your screen. Essentially select the document name to open the ZIP file.
- The Open file discourse box will open and you should review your downloaded document. Since the document is still in the ZIP group, you'll have to unquicken or extricate it first. Basically select the Extract all Files.
- You'll be solicited to determine the area from where you need to save the separated (unquickened) document. You can acknowledge the default area or select the Browse button to choose the area where you need the document saved. Select the Extract
- The Open file exchange box will open and you should review your recently changed over PDF to PNG document. You can open the document by double tapping on it if you simply need to perceive how the file looks. For the present, close the window by tapping on the red X.
- When you have your PDF changed over to PNG position, you'll need to transfer the PNG document to Cricut Design Space so you can exploit its Print Then Cut component.

Chapter Three: How To Work With Images And Edit Panel

Images

The Cricut Image Library has more than 50,000 images, being updated constantly. You don't have to claim a image to give it a shot—Cricut Design Space permits you to design with a image before you purchase so you can ensure it will work for the task.

Note: Available images may change by locale dependent on your private location and the authorizing understandings.

To get to the Cricut Image Library, from the left menu of the design screen, click "insert Images."

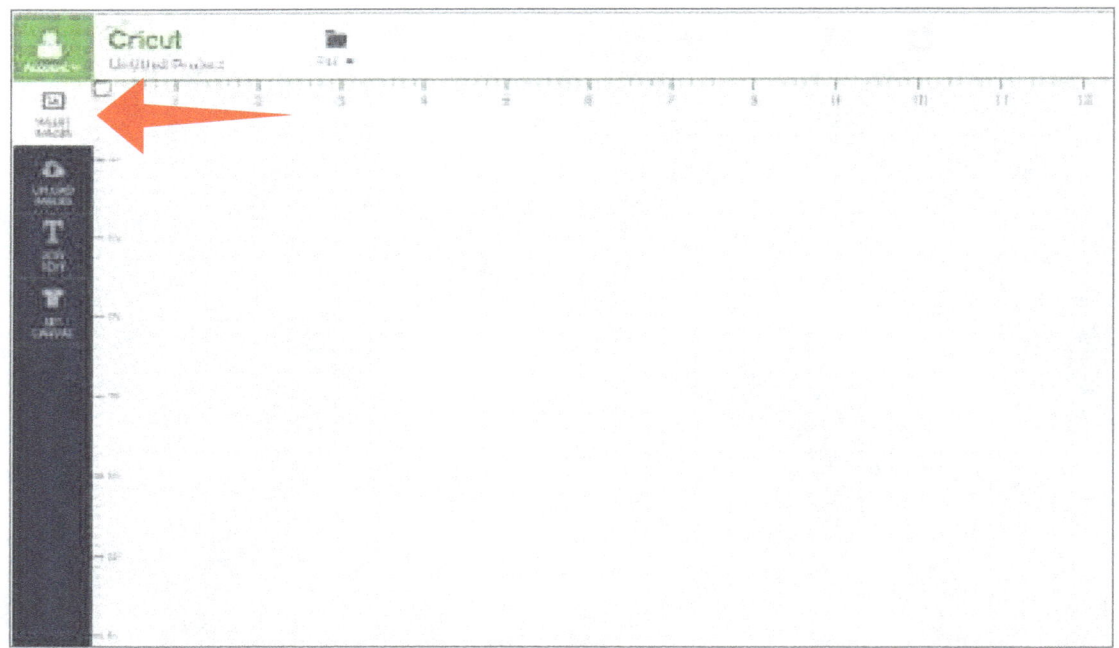

Another window opens so you can review and choose images from the Image Library. The Image Library incorporates Cricut images just as your own transferred images. Here you can search, read, and filter images.

On the upper left of the screen, there are three file choices: Cartridges, All Images, and Categories.

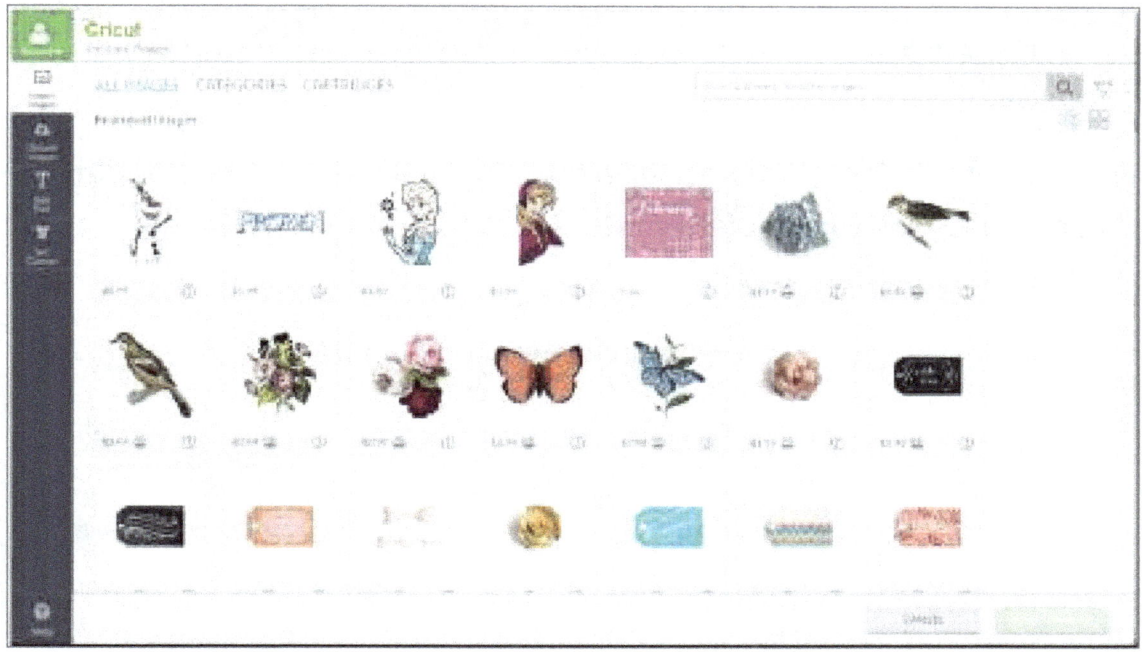

Inserting a image

Stage 2. On the screen you will discover an assortment of image tiles. Selecta image tile you might want to work with. A green check will show up on the tile and the image will be added to your image plate. You can include the same number of images as you like.

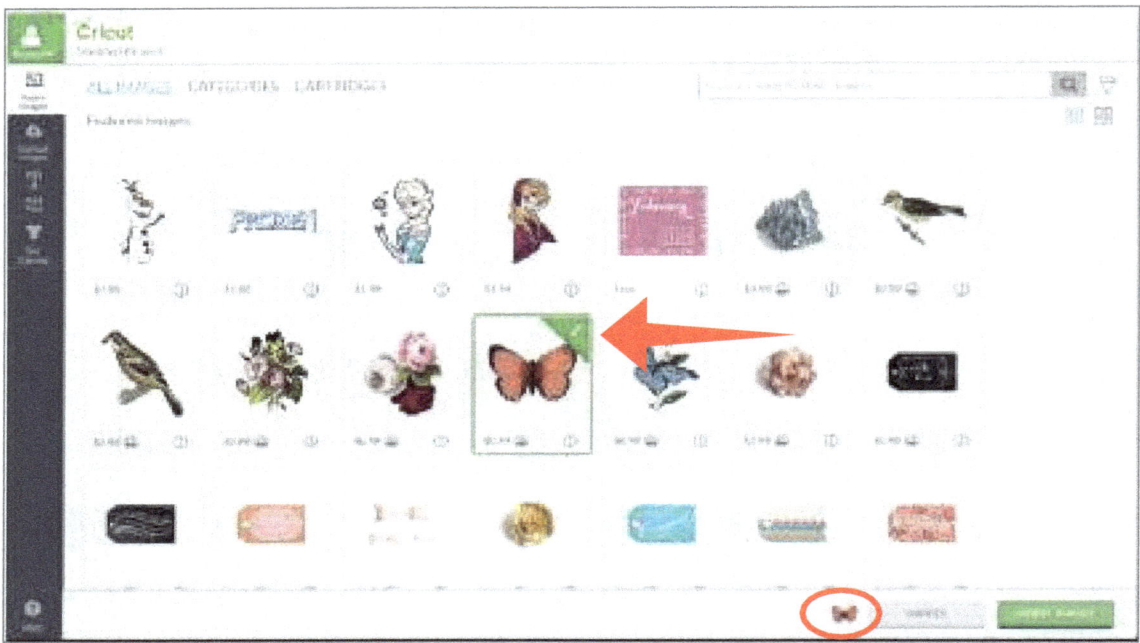

Tip: Find more data about a image by clicking the icon. You would now be able to review the name of the image, your degree of access, the image number, and the image set it has a place with (if accessible). You can likewise promptly buy the image, if you like.

If you might want to review extra images in the cartridge (image set), selectthe cartridge name to review the whole contribution. Images inside cartridges ordinarily have a comparative design feel.

Return to the image review, by tapping the symbol once more.

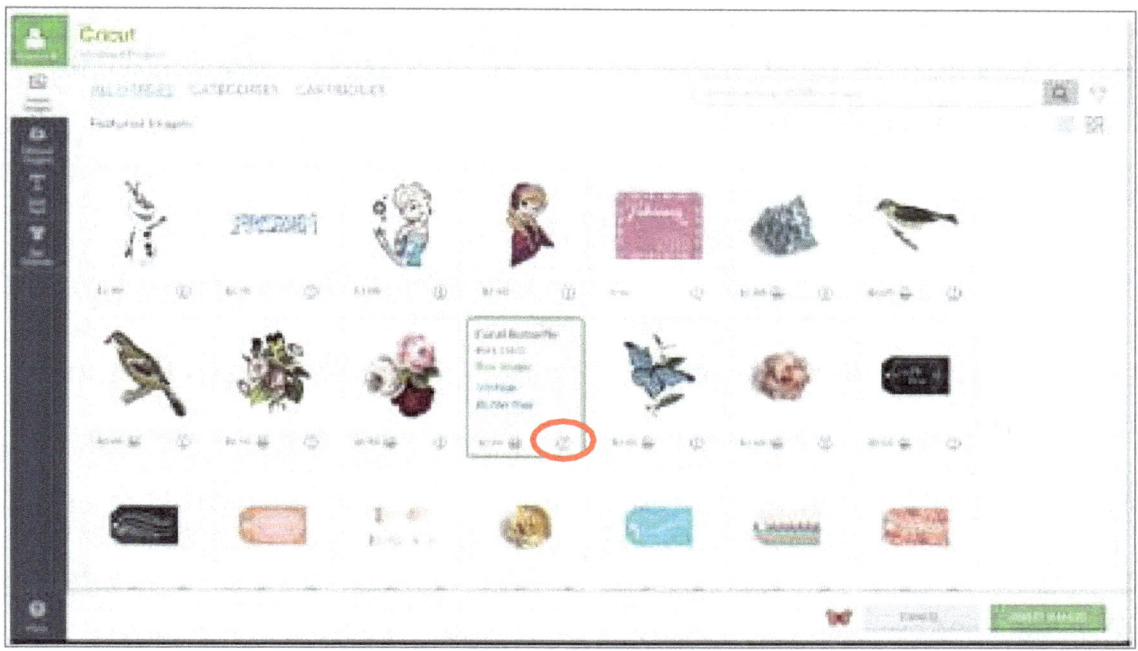

Stage 3. When images are chosen, click "Insert Images" to add them to the design screen.

Tip: Should there be a image in the design plate that you never again need, float over the image until a red "X" shows up. Tapping on the image will expel it from the image plate. Likewise, if you choose not to add any images to the design screen, you can click "Drop" in the base right corner of the screen.

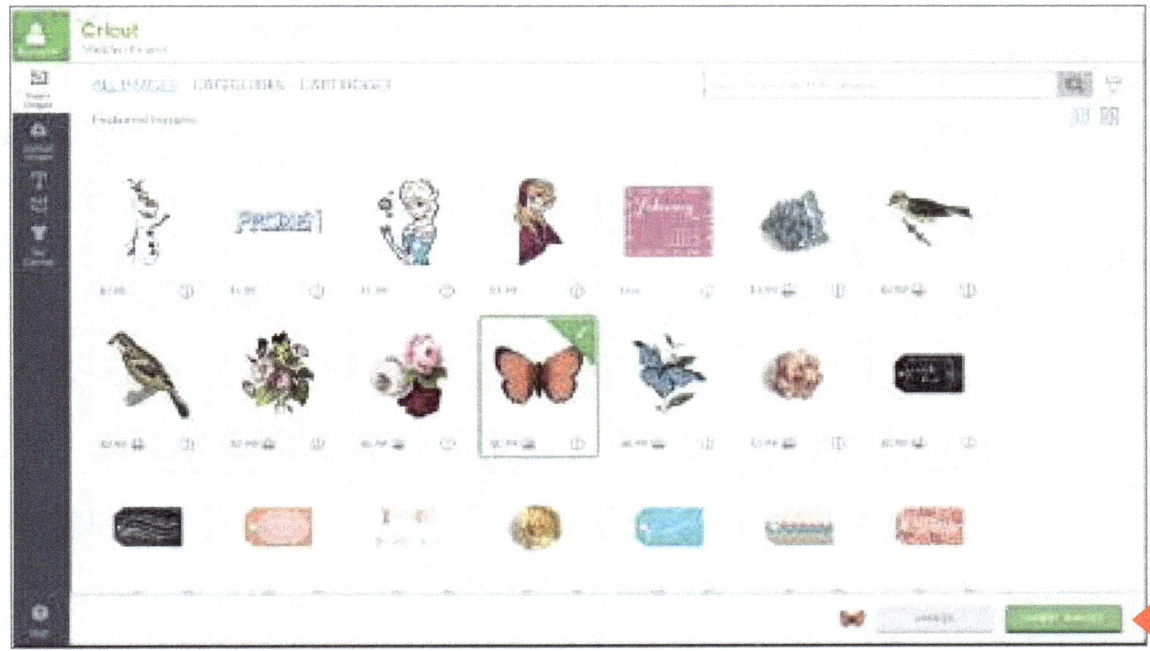

Stage 4. You would now be able to move and measure images to envision what they'll look like on your undertaking.

Image Search

The Cricut Image Library incorporates more than 50,000 images just as your own transferred images. Scanning for a particular watchword, expression, or cartridge (image set) will assist you with narrowing the image edits so you can locate the ideal image for your project.

Stage 1. To look by button phrase or expression, start by clicking "Insert Images" from the left menu of the structure screen to get to the Cricut® Image Library

Stage 2. Another window opens so you can review the Image Library. You will arrive on "All Images" file where you can start your inquiry.

• All Images: View included images or quest for a particular image

Stage 3. Type in a button phrase or expression into the hunt field and click the amplifying glass.

Tip: The image tally inside the pursuit box shows what number of images were found with your request.

Stage 4. Select an image tile to add it to your image plate or keep on looking for another image.

Stage 5. When images are chosen, click "Insert Images" to add them to the design screen.

Stage 6. You would now be able to move and estimate images to envision what they'll look like on your task.

Looking with channels

Use channels to foreheads images or tight your image indexed lists by proprietorship, type or layers.

Stage 1. To limit image decisions with channels, start by clicking "Insert Images" from the left menu of the structure screen to get to the Cricut® Image Library.

Stage 2. Another window opens so you can review the Image Library.

Stage 3. Select the Filter menu, on the upper right, to show the channel choices.

Stage 4. Select the kind of channel you might want to apply to the image review: Ownership, Type, or Layers. Proprietorship will channel the images dependent on your degree of access.

• My Images – Includes images that are free, transferred, connected, acquired, and part of a Cricut® Image Library membership design (if you are bought in).

• Uploaded – Includes images you have transferred to Cricut Design Space™.

• Free – Includes images that can be utilized without a buy.

• Subscription – Includes images that are a piece of the Cricut® Image Library membership (if you are bought in).

• Purchased – Includes cartridges that have been connected to your machine, just as images or computerized cartridges you have acquired.

Image Filters

Type will channel images dependent on the image style.

• 3D Objects – Includes images that are collapsed or sorted out to make boxes, blossoms, cupcake liners, and so forth.

• Backgrounds and Textures – Includes images that have a brightening design or example that fill most of the image.

• Borders – Includes images that work as an elaborate strip or design around the external edge of a image.

• Cards and Envelopes – Includes images that are collapsed to make a customized welcome card or envelope.

- Frames — Includes images with an enlivening outskirt and an open or strong focus.

- Phrases — Includes image designs that structure beautifying estimations.

- Printables — Includes images with enlivening examples and designs, which will print on your home printer and afterward be removed with your Cricut machine.

Layers will channel images dependent on the quantity of materials you need.

- Single Layer — Includes images that require just a single material to make.

- Multiple Layer — Includes images that require more than one material to make.

In the model beneath we applied the possession channel "Free."

Stage 5. Repeat the procedure to apply extra channels. You can apply the same number of channels as you like. In the model beneath we applied an extra channel, the sort channel "Cards and Envelopes."

Stage 6. The channel choices are fileed at the highest point of the screen. You can reject any of the channels by tapping on the "X". In the model beneath we rejected the "Free" channel.

Stage 7. Select an image tile to add it to your image plate or quest for another image.

Stage 8. When images are chosen, click "Insert Images" to add them to the design screen.

Stage 9. You would now be able to move and estimate images to envision what they'll look like on your task.

Browsing by image class

If you don't have a particular image as a main priority, you can search through classes to get thoughts from the Image Library.

Stage 1: To search images by class, start by clicking "Insert Images" from the left menu of the design screen to get to the Cricut® Image Library.

Stage 2: another window opens so you can review the Image Library.

Stage 3: To get to the image classes, select "Classifications" on the upper left half of the window. The screen changes to show a list of in excess of 50 image classes. Select an image classification by tapping on the tile.

Stage 4: The screen changes to show all images that have been labelled with this class. Select an image tile to add it to your image plate or quest for another image.

Tip: The class name will be spoken to in the upper left of the screen. Click the "X" by the classification name to search the full list of classes once more.

Stage 5: Once images are chosen, click "Insert Images" to add them to the structure screen.

Stage 6: You would now be able to move and measure images to envision what they'll look like on your project.

Browsing and Searching for Cartridges

While making a project, you may decide to utilize structures from cartridges (image sets). Images inside cartridges for the most part have a comparative design feel which can help cause your task to feel increasingly durable.

Stage 1. To review distinctive cartridge choices, start by getting to the Cricut Image Library. Click "Addition Images" from the left menu of the design screen.

Stage 2. Another window will open containing the Image Library. Selectthe Cartridges tab on the upper left of the screen to search an in sequential order list of more than 400 cartridges.

Stage 3. The view will change to incorporate a list of all Cricut cartridges, every one of which is spoken to by an even tile.

The cartridge tile gives you the cartridge name and an agent test of the images on the cartridge. On the correct side of the cartridge, you will review the quantity of images on that cartridge and your degree of access including Free, Purchased, Subscribed or a cost for procurement.

You can either look through the list of cartridges in sequential order request or quest for a particular cartridge. To look for a particular cartridge, type part or the whole cartridge name in the pursuit field and click the amplifying glass.

Tip: Purchasing a whole cartridge can be a huge cost reserve funds over buying singular images.

Stage 4. To show every one of the images found inside a cartridge, click "View All Images".

Stage 5. The view changes to show the whole of the images having a place with the cartridge. Here you can look and channel inside this particular cartridge. The text in the hunt bar demonstrates that you are looking through just inside this cartridge.

To look for a particular image in the cartridge, type the term in the inquiry bar and selectthe amplifying glass.

Stage 6. The outcomes show the images inside the cartridge that have been labeled with your hunt term. When images are chosen, click "Addition Images" to add them to the design screen.

Tip: View all images from the cartridge once more, by tapping the "X" in the inquiry field. Come back to search all cartridges, by tapping on the Cartridges list.

Stage 6: You would now be able to move and estimate images to envision what they'll look like on your task.

Transfer Images

Cricut Design Space™ enables you to utilize one of our 50,000+ Cricut® images or utilize your own images for nothing. Cricut® urges you to regard the protected innovation right of others and just transfer images you possess or are approved to utilize.

Utilizing the Cut What You Want® instrument in Design Space®, lets you transfer most .jpg, .bmp, .png, .gif, .svg and .dxf documents and changes over them into cuttable shapes. The instrument doesn't permit you to make editations to the structure itself.

There are two unique sorts of transfers: Basic and Vector. The procedure varies between file types dependent on how the documents are made and saved.

Essential Upload: The basic transfer process is utilized for .jpg, .bmp, .png, and .gif files. These documents are transferred as a solitary layer. To work with these sorts of files, the product takes you through a couple of basic undertakings to evacuate undesirable pieces of the image. When the procedure is finished, you can pick whether to print the image on your home printer and afterward cut it out (this is the default), cut around the edges of the image, or draw the edges of the image.

In the model beneath, you can pick between two choices:

(1) Use the print thenslice highlight to print the image on your home printer and cut around the edge utilizing your Cricut machine.

(2) Only cut or draw the outline of the image.

Vector Upload: The vector transfer process permits you to change over .svg and .dxf images into cuttable images. Multi-layered images will be saved as a composite image and afterward separated into layers on the design screen.

strong hues or strong colour files, laid out text, or layers. Notwithstanding, layered images ought to remain ungrouped.

Your transferred images likewise are accessible on the Insert Images screen. You can look by image name or tag, or you can choose "transferred" under the image channel.

Cricut configuration Space enables you to transfer and change over most .jpg, .bmp, .png and .gif images into cuttable shapes for nothing.

Stage 1: To start an essential transfer, click "Transfer Images" on the left half of the design screen.

Stage 2: A window will open which prompts you to pick your image document type. "Basic Upload" permits you to work with .jpg, .bmp, .png and .gif image documents. To start, pick "Transfer Image."

Transfer Images – Basic Upload

Stage 3: Click "Search" to discover the image you need to use from your PC. The document selector will open. Select the .jpg, .gif, .png, or .bmp file you need to transfer.

Stage 4: Choose if your image is essential, reasonably intricate, or complex dependent on the depictions found on the screen. Coordinating up the image that most intently lines up with your transferred image will assist you with bettering make the cut line. Click "Proceed".

Stage 5: In this progression, you'll characterize the cut lines of your image. Utilize the Crop, Selectand Delete, and Delete devices to expel the undesirable foundation from your image. The checker panel foundation demonstrates the zones, which have been expelled and won't cut. The strong zones speak to the image you will use on the structure screen.

A few devices assist you with tidying up your images by erasing undesirable regions.

Yield – Delete all regions that are not chosen when you drag the case over the image.

Selectand Delete – Delete the territories with comparable hues when you selectthem.

Eradicate – Delete territories by clicking and hauling the hover over the image. Utilize the slider to measure the deleter for better control.

In this model, a client would print the lion and cut around the edge.

Stage 6: Once you have evacuated the undesirable territories, select "Review" to show the cut lines of your image. They will be shown in red.

If the image doesn't show up as wanted, click "Review" again to come back to the editing view. At that point, keep on evacuating segments of the image until you are happy with the review.

Stage 7: Once the images is cleaned and lives up to your desires, click "Proceed".

Stage 8: Name your image and label it (whenever wanted) for simple looking. Choose if you need to safeguard the whole image for print, thencut. Sparing with the case checked will add the image to the design screen as a print thencut image.

Sparing with the case unchecked will save just the outside outline as the image cut way. Stage 9: When you are done, click "Save".

Stage 10: You will come back to the Upload Images window. The new image will show up in the Uploaded Images Library at the base of the screen. To add the image to your structure screen, selectyour image and a green check will show up demonstrating it is chosen. Thenclick the Insert Images button.

Tip: Your transferred images additionally are accessible on the Insert Images screen. You can look by image name or tag, or you can choose "transferred" under the image channel.

It would be ideal if you note: Cricut urges you to regard the licensed innovation privileges of others and just make duplicates of images you possess and are approved to utilize.

Transfer Images – Vector Upload

Cricut Design Space enables you to transfer and change over most .svg and .dxf petitions for nothing. Stage 1: To start a vector transfer, click "Transfer Images" on the left half of the design screen.

Tip: If you haven't as of now, you should sign in to your file.

Stage 2: A window will open which prompts you to pick your image file type. "Vector Upload" permits you to work with .svg or .dxf documents. To start, pick "Transfer Image."

Stage 3: Click "Search" to discover the image you need to use from your PC. The file selector will open. Selectthe .svg or .dxf document you need to transfer.

Tip: Cricut Design Space can work with files made from other design programming. The files can incorporate strong hues or strong colour fills, sketched out text, or layers. Nonetheless, if you have layered images, you ought to guarantee that the layers are ungrouped in the first file.

Stage 4: Name your image and label it (whenever wanted) for each looking and click "Save".

Stage 5: You will come back to the Upload Images window. The new image will show up in the Uploaded Images Library at the base of the screen. To add the image to your structure screen, selectyour image and a green check will show up demonstrating it is chosen. Then click the Insert Images button.

Tip: Your transferred images likewise are accessible on the "Supplement Images" screen. You can look by image name or tag, or you can choose "Transferred" as a proprietorship channel.

Stage 6: Vector images will show up on your design screen as an assembled image. If ungrouped, the image layers can be moved and measured independently.

If it's not too much trouble note: Cricut urges you to regard the protected innovation privileges of others and just make duplicates of images you possess and are approved to utilize.

Choosing a solitary image

If you wish to edit a image on the design screen, it must to be chosen. There are four different ways to choose a solitary image:

1. Selectby tapping on the image on the design screen

2. Selectthe image in the Layers panel

3. Selecta image by drawing a case

4. Selecta solitary image with the SelectAll button

Tip: When you selecta image, you selectthe whole of the layers that are assembled. If you might want to choose an individual layer, you should ungroup the image by clicking "Ungroup" on the base of the Layers Panel.

Choice 1: Selectby tapping on a image on the structure screen

Selectthe image on the structure screen to choose it. You will realize the image is chosen when a jumping box shows up and the image is featured in dark on the Layers panel.

Tip: To deselectthe image, click outside the jumping box.

Choice 2: Selecta image in the Layers panel

Click the name of the image in the Layers panel. This will likewise choose the image on the structure screen.

Choice 3: Selecta image by drawing a case

Draw a case around the image by clicking outside the image and afterward holding while you drag a case totally over the image you might want to choose.

Tip: The image must be totally inside the blue box with the end goal for it to be chosen.

Choice 4: Selecta solitary image with the SelectAll button

If you just have one image on your screen, you can choose it by tapping the SelectAll button at the highest point of the structure screen.

Tip: If more than one image is on the design screen, tapping the SelectAll button will choose every one of the images on the screen.

When images have been added to the structure screen, the images should be chosen so as to make edits. You can decide to choose an individual image or choose a few images without a moment's delay. Choosing images together permits you to move, estimate and pivot them simultaneously. There are three different ways to choose numerous images without a moment's delay:

1. Selectby tapping on the images on the design screen

2. Selectthe images in the Layers panel

3. Selectan image by drawing a case

Choice 1: Selectby tapping on the images on the design screen

Selectthe main image so the bouncing box shows up. Without declick oning that image, hold down the Shift key on your console and selectdifferent images you wish to choose. The jumping box will develop as images are chosen and the images are featured in dark on the Layers panel. Proceed with the procedure until every single wanted image are chosen.

Tip: To deselectevery one of the images, selecta clear region of the design screen.

Choice 2: Selectimages in the Layers panel

Click the name of the primary image in the Layers panel. This will likewise choose the image on the design screen. Holding down the Control button on your PC (Command key on your Mac), click the names of different images you wish to choose.

Choice 3: Selectimages drawing a crate.

Draw a crate around the images by clicking outside the images and afterward holding while you drag a container totally over the images you might want to choose.

Tip: The images must be totally inside the blue box with the goal for them to be chosen.

Tip: Click oning different images and Grouping images are basicly the same as. Be that as it may, choosing different images incidentally permits you to edit the images simultaneously. Each image will require choice each time you need to move, size, or turn it. Group images makes different images go about as a solitary image. When a group is chosen, all images or layers are accessible for edit and can immediately be move measured or turned. To make a image group, selectthe images you need assembled and click the Group button at the base of the Layers panel.

Image bouncing box

The jumping box is the case that shows up around your image when it is chosen. Each edge of the bouncing box permits you to cause a quick to edit.

- Top left – delete the image

- Top right – turn the image

- Bottom right – resize the image

- Bottom left – lock/open the image extents for measuring

To review the bouncing box, selectthe image.

Delete – Remove the image from the structure screen by tapping on the red "X" in the upper left corner of the bouncing box. The image will never again show up on the design screen and will be deleted from the Layers panel.

Turn – Click and hold the round bolt symbol in the upper right corner of the bouncing box and drag it toward any path. As you drag the pivot handle, a point marker shows up in the dark box by the bolt symbol.

Tip: Image pivots on the structure screen are for representation just and won't be pondered the mat review except if you join different turned images to another layer. If you might want to turn your image for cutting, do as such on the mat review.

Bolted extents – The shut lock symbol on the base left corner of the bouncing box demonstrates you will change the width and stature at a consistent proportion, keeping the image relative.

Size: To estimate the image with bolted extents, click and hold the blue bolt symbol on the base right corner of the jumping box and drag it slantly. As you make changes, the image size will be mirrored in the dark box beside the bolt symbol.

Opened extents The open lock symbol on the base left corner of the bouncing box demonstrates you will change the width and tallness of the image autonomous of one another.

Size – To measure the image with the extents opened, click and hold the green compass symbol on the base right corner of the bouncing box and drag toward any path. Hauling the symbol legitimately left or right changes just the width. Hauling the symbol here and there changes just the tallness. You likewise can drag the symbol askew to change that tallness and width simultaneously without holding a steady size proportion.

Measuring an image

Cricut Design Space permits you to slice or attract images up to 11.5" x 23.5" and print then slice images up to 6" x 8.5" (Print then cut measuring may differ contingent upon your program, Chrome can just estimate print then cut at 5.5" x 8").

The bouncing box around the image characterizes the image size. Width is the length of the most extensive focuses the even way while the stature is the length of the further focuses on the vertical bearing. At the point when a image is turned, the width and stature stay consistent.

When measuring a image, you can keep the size proportion steady with the goal that the length and width remain relative, or you can estimate the length and width exclusively.

There are two choices for estimating a image with a consistent size proportion which keeps the image extents. Choice 1: Size the image utilizing the jumping box

Stage 1 Selectthe image with the goal that the bouncing box shows up.

Stage 2 Click the bolt symbol on the base right corner of the bouncing box, and drag it slantingly to make the image bigger or littler. As you make changes, the image size will be mirrored in the dim box beside the bolt symbol.

When image measuring is finished, the Edit Panel will refresh to mirror the new size of the image.

Tip: If the lock symbol on the base left of the bouncing box is shut; as you drag the bolt the proportion among tallness and width will stay steady and the image will keep in extent.

Choice 2: Size the image utilizing the Edit Panel for explicit size necessities

Stage 1 Selectthe image with the goal that the jumping box shows up. When your image is chosen, you will review the size mirrored in the Edit Panel.

Stage 2 Click in the case by Width or Length and type in your particular size. You additionally can utilize the bolts to increment or lessening the size in 0.1" increases. The shut lock symbol shows that the width and length will change at a consistent size apportion keeping the image in extent.

There are two different ways to measure a image one way in particular, changing the image extents. Choice 1 Size the image utilizing the jumping box

Stage 1 Selectthe image with the goal that the bouncing box shows up.

Stage 2 Selectthe lock symbol on the base left corner of the bouncing box. The bouncing box will demonstrate that you can change the sizes separately. The lock symbol will give off an impression of being opened, and the bolt symbol for measuring the image will change to green.

Stage 3 Selectand hold the green bolt symbol while you drag it toward any path. Drag the symbol legitimately left or right to change just the width; or drag it here and there to change just the tallness. You additionally can drag the symbol corner to corner to change that tallness and width simultaneously without holding a steady size proportion.

Choice 2 Size the image utilizing the Edit Panel for explicit size prerequisites

Stage 1 Selectthe image with the goal that the bouncing box shows up. When your image is chosen, the size is appear in the Edit panel.

Stage 2 Selectthe lock symbol under size in the Edit Panel. The lock symbol will presently reviewm, by all accounts, to be opened, and will demonstrate that you can change the length and width separately.

Stage 3 Click in the crate by Width or Length and type in your particular size. You additionally can utilize the bolts to increment or abatement the size in 0.1" increases. The open lock symbol demonstrates that changes to width or stature will change autonomously.

Turning a image

Revolution assists with situating your images on the structure screen so you can imagine your undertaking. All images are added to the design screen at the 0 degree revolution. Images then can be pivoted in one-degree augments somewhere in the range of 0 and 360 degrees.

Tip: Image pivots on the structure screen are for representation just and won't be pondered the mat review except if you connect the turned image to another layer. If you might want to pivot your image for cutting, do as such on the mat review.

There are two choices for turning images on the structure screen:

1. Turning utilizing the bouncing box

2. Turning utilizing the Edit panel

Utilizing the bouncing box permits you to uninhibitedly change the pivot of the image by hauling, while changing the turn edge in the Edit panel lets you type in a particular edge.

Choice 1: Rotating utilizing the jumping box

Stage 1 Selectthe image with the goal that the bouncing box shows up.

Stage 2 Click and hold the round bolt symbol in the upper right corner of the bouncing box and drag it toward any path. As you make changes, the image turn will be mirrored in the dark edge pointer close to the image.

When image pivot is finished, the Edit Panel will refresh to mirror the new edge of the image.

Tip: If you don't care for the aftereffects of the revolution, the Undo button can securely fix any progressions you make.

Choice 2: Rotating utilizing the Edit panel

Stage 1 Selectthe image with the goal that the jumping box shows up.

Stage 2 In the Edit panel, click in the Rotate field and type in a particular size. You likewise can tap the bolts to increment or lessening the edge in one-degree increases.

Tip: If you don't care for the aftereffects of the turn, the Undo button can fix any progressions you make.

Cricut Design Space permits you to flip the course of a image vertically or on a flatten designe on the structure screen utilizing the Mirror quickens in the Layers panel.

Choice 1: Mirror on a flatten designe

Stage 1 Selectthe image so the bouncing box shows up.

Stage 2 To mirror on a flatten designe, click the left button under "Mirror" in the Edit Panel. Turn of the image will stay at 0 degrees. Click the button again to come back to the first position.

Tip: While changes in revolution don't show up on the mat review, mirrored images on the structure screen will hold changes on the mat review.

Choice 2 Mirror vertically

Stage 1 Selectthe image with the goal that the jumping box shows up.

Stage 2 To mirror vertically, click the correct button under "Mirror" in the Edit Panel. Pivot of the image will change to 180 degrees. Click the button again to come back to the first position.

Tip: If you intend to cut iron-on, complete your structure on the design screen first. You would then be able to mirror each mat of your design exclusively on the mat review by checking the "Mirror (for iron-on)" check box.

Copying a image

There are two different ways to copy a image on the design screen:

1. Reordering

2. Copying on the Layers panel

Tip: If you might want to make numerous duplicates of the whole task, on the mat review change the quantity of undertaking duplicates and click "Apply".

Choice 1: Copying and gluing

Stage 1 Selectthe image with the goal that the jumping box shows up.

Stage 2 Click the Copy button (situated in the top menu) to duplicate the image to your clippanel.

Stage 3 Click the Paste button (situated in the top menu) to glue the image from your clippanel. A duplicate of the image will be added to the structure screen and will show up marginally balance from the first image. The new image likewise will be appeared in the Layers panel.

Choice 2: Duplicating on the Layers panel

Stage 1 Selectthe image with the goal that the jumping box shows up.

Stage 2 Click the Duplicate button at the base of the Layers panel. A second duplicate of the image will show up marginally balance from the first image. The new image additionally will be appeared in the Layers panel.

Erasing an image

If a image is insertded and later is never again required, there are three different ways to delete the image from the design screen.

- Delete a image utilizing the bouncing box
- Delete a image utilizing the Layers panel
- Delete a image utilizing the delete key on your PC console

Tip: You can conceal a image from the structure screen if you would prefer not to forever delete it from the project. Images that are shrouded won't be sent to the mat review for cutting.

Choice 1 Delete a image utilizing the jumping box

Stage 1 Selectthe image so the bouncing box shows up.

Stage 2 To delete the image, click the red "X" in the upper left corner of the jumping box.

Choice 2 Delete a image utilizing the Layers panel

Stage 1 Selectthe image with the goal that the jumping box shows up.

Stage 2 To delete the image, click the rubbish can symbol at the base of the Layers Panel.

Choice 3 Delete a image utilizing delete key on your PC console Step 1 Selectthe image so the jumping box shows up.

Stage 2 To delete the image, click the "Delete" key on your PC console.

Group permits you to move, size, and turn images as one article. At the point when images are grouped, it is just for accommodation when working with images on the structure screen. Groups won't change how the image shows up on the cutting mat. You can assemble singular layers or numerous images.

At the point when you insert multi-layered images to the structure screen, the layers of that image are assembled.

At the point when you selectthe image on the structure screen, the whole of the layers will be featured in dark on the Layers panel, demonstrating that it is an assembled image.

Tip: There are some individual layer edits you can do inside a grouped image or assembled set of images. These edits incorporate changing the layer colour, changing the layer line type, and concealing a layer.

If you might want to work with singular layers, you should ungroup the image. When the image is chosen on the structure screen, click the Ungroup button at the base of the Layers panel.

The individual layers would now be able to be moved, measured and turned independently. The layers will appear as separated groups inside the Layers panel.

To refocus the layers, selectthe two layers on the structure screen and afterward click "Group" at the base of the Layers panel.

The new assembled image will be mirrored in the Layers panel.

Group different images

You can bunch different images so you can move, resize and turn the images without a moment's delay. The Layers panel shows that there are two grouped images on the design screen.

To bunch the images, selectthe two images on the structure screen. A bouncing box will show up around both of the images. At that point, click the Group button at the base of the Layers panel.

The Layers panel will mirror that the images are a piece of one group.

Tip: Ungrouping a lot of grouped images will return you to the individual assembled images. If you might want to work with the individual layers, you should ungroup a subsequent time.

Covering up and unhiding image layers

In Cricut Design Space™, you have the choice to stow away or unhide a layer. At the point when a layer is unmistakable or unhidden, it will show up in the layers panel with an eye symbol. At the point when a layer is covered up, it won't show up on the structure screen or cut with your last undertaking; be that as it may, it will show up in the Layers panel with a crossed-out eye symbol.

Numerous Cricut images have pre-concealed layers (regularly shadows) when added to the design screen. You can unhide these layers in the Layers panel.

Stage 1: Selectthe eye symbol in the layer band on the Layers panel.

Stage 2: The symbol will change to a crossed-out eye, the layer never again will show up on the design screen and, it won't cut with the last project.

Stage 1: Selectthe crossed-out eye symbol in the layer band of the Layers panel.

Stage 2: The symbol will change to an eye, and the layer will presently show up on the undertaking.

Choosing a line type

The line type decides whether the layer or text will cut, score, write or print thencut in your last project. It is spoken to by an image by the layer thumbnail. Line type is recognized on the Layers panel with a Line Type symbol. You can change Line type from the Layers panel by getting to the Line Type flyout.

Cut – The image will be cut from your material.

Write – The image will be drawn utilizing a Cricut® pen.

Score – The image will score utilizing a Cricut® Scoring Stylus.

Print thenCut – The image will be printed utilizing your home printer and afterward cut on your Cricut® machine.

Stage 1: Click the line type symbol or layer thumbnail in the Layers panel to open the line type flyout. A blue line under the choice will show the present line type.

Tip: The line sort of each layer must be changed independently.

Stage 2: Click the symbol that speaks to the ideal line type. The image line type on the structure screen will change to mirror changes in the Layers panel. At the point when you are finished with your choices, click outside the line type flyout to close it.

Tip: If there are different layers to your task and the line type is set to write or score, the image should be attached to another layer by choosing the two layers and tapping the Attach button in the Layers panel.

Changing the colour of cut layers

Choosing hues for singular image layers encourages you envision your last task, yet additionally decides how images are spread out on the cutting mats. Images are separated and put on the mats dependent on colour; layers with a similar colour are situated on similar mats.

There are three different ways to utilize the Line Type flyout to choose new hues for cut and print layers.

1. Basic colour swatches

2. Custom colour picker

3. Hex qualities

You can likewise utilize the Sync panel to decrease the quantity of cutting mats required in a project.

Tip: You can change singular layer hues inside a grouped image without ungrouping the image.

Choice 1: Basic colour swatches

To rapidly choose a colour, utilize one of the 30 essential hues offered in the basic colour swatches. Stage 1: Click the layer thumbnail in the Layers panel.

You'll locate the essential colour swatches hanging in the balance Type flyout.

Stage 2: Selecta colour by tapping on one of the essential colour swatches. The new colour is pondered the design screen and in the Layers panel.

Click outside of the Line Type flyout to close it.

Changing the colour of cut layers

Choice 2: Custom colour picker

You have a lot more colour choices for your designs when you utilize the custom colour picker. Stage 1: Click the layer thumbnail in the Layers panel.

You'll locate the custom colour picker hanging in the balance Type flyout.

Stage 2: Move the vertical slider up or down to change the colour over the range. The new colour is considered the design screen and in the Layers panel.

Tip: If you are attempting to coordinate a particular material colour, have a go at picking the basic colour that is nearest to your material colour. This will place you in the inexact colour range. You would then be able to keep on refining the colour match utilizing the custom colour picker.

Stage 3: Selecta particular tone inside the colour family by moving the hover inside the square colour region.

Clicking outside of the Line Type flyout to will close it.

Choice 3: Hex qualities

Hex qualities are codes that speak to colour. The six-digit Hex worth may incorporate numbers, letter, or a blend of both. In the custom colour picker, Hex qualities permit you to choose a quite certain colour for your images.

Stage 1: Click the layer thumbnail in the Layers panel.

The Line Type flyout shows up and shows the hex worth field where you can enter the hex code.

Changing the colour of cut layers

Stage 2: Type the six-digit hex an incentive into the field at the base of the Line Type flyout. The new colour is thought about the structure screen and in the Layers panel.

Click outside of the line type panel to close it.

Tip: The Colour Sync device makes it simple to apply custom hues to numerous layers inside a task. When the colour has been applied to one layer, open the Colour Sync panel and move extra layers to that colour.

Changing colour for images with a print Line Type

Choosing hues for singular image layers causes you imagine your last project, yet in addition decides how images are spread out on the cutting mats. For Print the Cut images, the colour on the design screen mirrors the colour that will be utilized when you print the images.

All progressions to layer hues should be made before straightening the image. If you might want to change the colour of a smoothed image, you should unflatten it first.

There are three different ways to choose new hues for images with a print Line Type.

1. Basic colour swatches

2. Custom colour picker

3. Hex qualities

Tip: You can change singular layer hues inside an assembled image without ungrouping the image as long as the layers aren't straightened together.

Choice 1 Basic colour swatches

To rapidly choose a colour of a image layer with a print Line Type, utilize one of the 30 basic hues offered in the essential colour swatches.

Stage 1: Click the layer thumbnail in the Layers panel.

You'll locate the essential colour swatches hanging in the balance Type flyout.

Stage 2: Selecta colour by tapping on one of the essential colour swatches. The new colour is pondered the design screen and in the Layers panel. Click outside of the Line Type flyout to close it.

Tip: Once you are finished changing the hues, you can straighten the image into one layer for printing. Click "Flatten" on the Layers panel.

Choice 2 Custom colour picker

You have a lot more colour choices for your structures when you utilize the custom colour picker. Stage 1: Click the layer thumbnail in the Layers p

You'll locate the custom colour picker hanging in the balance Type flyout.

Changing colour for images with a print Line Type

Stage 2: Move the vertical slider up or down to change the colour over the range. The new colour is considered the design screen and in the Layers panel.

Stage 3: Selecta particular tint inside the colour family by moving the hover inside the square colour zone. Click outside of the Line Type flyout to close it.

Tip: Once you are finished changing the hues, you can straighten the image into one layer for printing. Click "Smooth" on the Layers panel.

Changing colour for images with a print Line Type

Choice 3 Hex qualities

Hex qualities are codes that speak to colour. The six-digit hex worth may incorporate numbers, letters, or a blend of both. In the custom colour picker, hex qualities permit you to choose a quite certain colour for your images.

Stage 1: Click the layer thumbnail in the Layers panel.

The Line Type flyout shows up and shows the hex worth field where you can enter the hex code.

Stage 2: Type the six-digit hex an incentive into the field at the base of the Line Type flyout. The new colour is considered the design screen and in the Layers panel. Click outside of the line type panel to close it once more.

Tip: Once you are finished changing the hues, you can choose different layers and straighten the image into one layer for printing. Click "Straighten" on the Layers panel.

Choosing the pen colour for write layers

Utilize the writing highlight of Cricut Explore® machines to draw an enlivening component or write message on your project. Cricut Design Space™ permits you to change the colour of the image or text on the screen to coordinate the pen colour you will use in your machine. This will assist you with imagining your last task. The machine will provoke you when to utilize the pen and what colour of pen to utilize. The colour choices mirror the Cricut Explore® pens accessible for procurement. The name of the pen colour can be found on the barrel of the pen.

Stage 1: Click the layer thumbnail in the Layers Panel.

The Line Type flyout shows up and shows a list of pen hues, with the present colour featured in dim.

Tip: The colour list arranges with Cricut Explore® pen hues; the name of the colour is fileed on the pen barrel. Make a point to choose the right pen colour structure the Line Type flyout. You will be incited to insert the proper pen colour preceding starting the writing procedure.

Stage 2: Click the colour swatch of the new colour you might want to use in your task. The new colour is thought about the design screen and is featured in dim on hold Type flyout.

Clicking outside of the Line Type flyout closes it.

Tip: If your image is set to an choice line type, you should tap the Write tab on hold Type flyout before choosing a pen colour.

Colour adjusting images

The Sync Panel encourages you merge hues inside your project to lessen the quantity of various materials you intend to utilize, in this way decreasing the quantity of cutting mats required for an undertaking. When synchronizing hues, you can change a solitary layer independently or all layers of a particular colour without a moment's delay.

Tip: Images are separated and set on the mats dependent on colour; layers with a similar colour are situated on similar mats. If you have layers with even somewhat various hues, they will cut on various mats. Utilize the Sync Panel to solidify minor departure from a solitary colour.

Changing a solitary layer colour separately

Stage 1: Selectthe Sync tab to open the Sync panel.

The panel shows your layers arranged by colour.

Stage 2: Drag a layer thumbnail to an choice colour.

The layer thumbnail will move to the new colour and the change will be thought about the design screen.

Tip: If you wish to turn around the progressions you've made, click the "Fix" button on the top menu to return a stage. You can click "Fix" a few times to return a few stages.

Changing a colour line to an choice colour

Stage 1: Selectthe Sync tab to open the Sync panel.

The panel review shows your layers arranged by colour.

Stage 2: Selectthe colour bar on the left half of the line and hold while hauling that colour bar to a choice colour. The column will feature in dim to show that it has been chosen.

The whole of the tiles from the line will move to the new colour and the progressions will be pondered the structure screen.

The position highlight of the Edit panel lets you absolutely position images on the structure screen. This element is especially helpful when adjusting different images along the left or top. Position is constantly estimated from the upper left corner of the design screen to the upper left corner of the jumping box.

X position – the flat situation of the image

Y position – the vertical situation of the image

At the point when a image is moved, a dim box shows up demonstrating both the X and Y position in the structure screen. When you have wrapped up the image, the position will refresh in the Edit panel.

There are two choices for arrangement with image position.

1. Top arrangement

2. Left arrangement

Tip: Positions on the design screen won't influence the manner in which images are spread out on the mat except if you utilize the Attach apparatus.

Choice 1: Using position to top adjust images

Stage 1: Insert images you'd prefer to top-adjust to the design screen.

Stage 2: Selecta image you might want use as a source of perspective for top arrangement and afterward note the "Y" position

Stage 3: Use the Y position directions of the arrangement image to coordinate the situation of extra images so they are in succession. Repeat to top-adjust different images in different positions.

Stage 1: Insert images you'd prefer to left-adjust to the structure screen.

Stage 2: Selecta image you might want to use as a source of perspective for left arrangement and afterward note the "X" position.

Stage 3: Use the X position directions of the arrangement image to coordinate the situation of extra images with the goal that they show up in a segment. Repeat to left-adjust different images in different positions.

Organizing images

During the structure procedure, you may need to modify the request for layers from front to back. Masterminding permits you to change the request in which images or layers show up on the structure screen by pushing images and layers ahead and in reverse.

Layer request can be thought of as a deck of cards. Think about the layers of a image or project as the individual cards. You can undoubtedly move the base card to the center or the highest point of the deck, and the top card to the center or base of the deck. This is the thing that you can do with your images and layers with arrangement included.

Utilize the Layers panel as a manual for review the request for your layers. Images in the Layers panel reviewm stacked as per the pattern in which they show up on the structure screen. The base layer of the panel is additionally the base layer of the task; then again, the top layer of the panel is the top layer of your project. Just one grouped image or each layer can be masterminded in turn.

Tip: When utilizing the mastermind include, assembled images will move all together. If you need to change the request for only one layer of a image, the image should be ungrouped. Ungrouping a image will carry all layers to the highest point of the task.

Tip: When a layer is copied or reordered, its duplicate will turn into the top layer of the project.

Move images or layers utilizing the accompanying activities:

- Move to Back – Send the chose image or layer to the rear of the stacking request.
- Move Backward – Move the chose image or layer one layer in reverse in the stacking request.
- Move Forward – Move the chose image or layer one layer forward in the stacking request.
- Move to Front – Bring the chose image or layer to the front of the stacking request.

Choice 1: Move to back

Stage 1: Selectthe image you wish to arrange.

Stage 2: Open the Arrange menu and select"Move to Back."

Stage 3: The image moves from its present put in the request to the base layer of the structure. This change is additionally mirrored in the Layers panel. (The yellow hover beneath was moved to more readily show stacking request.)

Choice 2: Move Backward

Stage 1: Selectthe image you wish to mastermind.

Masterminding images

Stage 2: Open the Arrange menu and select "Go in reverse."

Stage 3: The image moves from its present submit in the request back one layer. This change is likewise mirrored in the Layers panel. (The blue hover beneath was moved to more readily represent stacking request.)

Arranging images

Edit 3: Move Forward

Stage 1: Select the image you wish to arrange.

Stage 2: Open the Arrange menu and select "Move forward."

Stage 3: The image moves from its present put in the request forward one layer. This change is likewise mirrored in the Layers panel. (The purple hover beneath was moved to all the more likely delineate stacking request.)

Choice 4: Move to Front

Stage 1: Select the image you wish to mastermind.

Stage 2: Open the Arrange menu and select "Move to Front."

Stage 3: The image moves from its present submit in the request to the top layer. This change is additionally mirrored in the Layers panel. (The red hover beneath was moved to all the more likely show stacking request.)

Designing for position on the mat

As a rule, projects are cut in paper saver mode, so images are consequently put on the cutting mat as near one another as conceivable to ration material. If you wish to hold your cuts in position with the goal that images on the cutting mat show up precisely as they appear on the design canvas, you can structure straightforwardly on the mat utilizing an essential canvas and the Attach device.

Stage 1: Select "Set Canvas" from the design screen to review accessible undertaking canvas types.

Stage 2: Select "Essential Canvas."

Stage 3: You will be reclaimed to the structure screen and the project canvas will be obvious out of sight. The canvas speaks to your mat yet won't cut. Utilizing the canvas panel, resize the canvas to the greatest size that can be cut on the mat.

Tip: For a 12" x 12" mat, the greatest cut size is 11.5" x 11.5". For a 12" x 24" mat, the most extreme cut size is 11.5" x 23.5".

Stage 4: Click the Grid On/Off catch to actuate the design screen lattice.

Stage 5: Create your project, situating every one of the images inside the canvas.

Stage 6: Select every one of the images you might want to hold position by colour, they will all be cutting from a similar mat.

Tip: You may wish to situate images with more than one colour, to work with the images you should ungroup before attaching. The Attach device will change over every chose layer into a solitary colour that will be cut from a similar mat. When layers have been connected, they would then be able to be grouped with different layers without affecting the manner in which the task cuts on the mat.

Stage 7: Click the Attach button on the Layers panel to hold the chose images set up.

Tip: If you might want to edit position after images have been joined, you can disengage them by clicking "Separate" in the Layers panel.

Stage 8: You will realize that your images are joined in light of the fact that they will show up as an attached set in the Layers panel. At the point when you are prepared to start the cutting procedure, click "Go."

Stage 9: The images are shown on the Mat review screen precisely as you have arranged them on the design screen. Click "Go" and afterward follow the on screen prompts to cut your undertaking.

Tip: If things are not joined, Cricut Design Space will cut in paper saver mode, which means it will consequently put articles on the cutting mat as near one another as conceivable to moderate material.

Utilizing numerous materials on a mat

Now and then when you are making a task it can appear to be monotonous to utilize a few mats to cut your undertaking. This can be helped by setting littler bits of material on the mat where the cuts will happen.

Stage 1: Select"Set Canvas" from the structure screen to review accessible project canvas types.

Stage 2: Select"Fundamental Canvas."

Stage 3: You will be reclaimed to the design screen and the task canvas will be unmistakable out of sight. The canvas speaks to your mat however won't cut. Utilizing the canvas panel, resize the canvas to the most extreme size that can be cut on the mat.

Tip: For a 12" x 12" mat, the most extreme cut size is 11.5" x 11.5". For a 12" x 24" mat, the most extreme cut size is 11.5" x 23.5".

Stage 4: Click the Grid On/Off catch to initiate the structure screen network.

Stage 5: Insert a multi-layer image to your design screen. Resize as wanted.

Stage 6: Selectthe image and click "Ungroup" to separate the layers. You will realize the image is ungrouped when the various layers are separated on the Layers panel.

Stage 7: Move the different layers to various areas of the undertaking canvas. Pieces that ought to be cut from a similar material ought to be situated in a similar segment.

Tip: Arranging the different layers in the four corners of the task canvas makes material position simpler.

Stage 8: Click "SelectAll" to choose all the various layers.

Stage 9: Click "Join" in the Layers panel to hold the situation on the canvas. This turns all images a similar colour so they will cut on a similar mat. This will likewise put images on the mat as appeared on the design screen.

Tip: Place materials on the cutting mat, utilizing the colour of the images and the network on the design screen as a guide.

Stage 10: When you are prepared to start the cutting procedure, click "Go."

Tip: Even however the colour of the layers reviewms, by all accounts, to be the equivalent on the canvas, the layers will be the colour of the materials you place your mat.

Stage 11: The images show up on the Mat review screen precisely as you have arranged them on the design screen. Click "Go" and afterward follow the onscreen prompts to cut your undertaking.

Cutting images

The Slice instrument parts two covering images or text into various parts. Cut makes another cut way from two images, bringing about at least two totally new shapes. Every one of the new shapes will appear in the Layers panel as an individual layer.

You can utilize the Slice device to remove a shape from another shape, cut covering shapes from each other or to cut text from a shape.

When utilizing Slice with images, you can just work with two layers one after another. If you are utilizing a multi-layered image, you can either stow away or ungroup different layers to initiate the Slice instrument. At the point when the Slice work is performed with concealed layers, every single concealed layer are expelled from the structure screen and the Layers panel. If you might want to utilize the image layers with your project, ungroup when utilizing the Slice apparatus.

Text works somewhat better with the Slice device. If text is multi-layered and one layer is covered up, you can utilize the Slice instrument. Nonetheless, if you ungroup text, it turns into a image and will never again work with the Slice device except if the text is ungrouped to singular letters.

Stage 1: Arrange the images with the goal that they are covering.

Stage 2: Selectthe two images by holding the Control key for PC or Command key for macintosh on your console while tapping on each layer.

A jumping box shows up around the two images, and the individual layers are featured in dark on the Layers panel. When two layers are chosen, the Slice symbol gets dynamic.

Stage 3: Click "Cut" at the highest point of the Layers Panel. The top layer assumes the colour of the base layer. The new images are mirrored in the Layers panel as cut images. Any concealed layers are expelled from the Layers panel.

Tip: When images incompletely cover, you will wind up with in excess of two new shapes. The specific number of shapes will rely upon the quantity of covers between the two chose images.

Stage 4: Separate the layers to audit your new shapes. Edit or delete the images separately.

Welding Images

The Weld device joins various shapes to make a solitary edited image, expelling any covering cut lines. This can be an incredible method to streamline a structure or join shapes to make new designs.

Stage 1: Move the images you might want to weld with the goal that they cover.

Tip: If you are working with multi-layered images, you may need to ungroup the layers to arrange them independently before welding.

Stage 2 Selectall images that will be welded together. When at least two layers are chosen, the Weld device will get dynamic.

Stage 3: Click "Weld" at the highest point of the Layers panel

The images are currently consolidated. Any place cut ways have converged, just the outside cut way remains. The welded image would now be able to be edited similarly as some other single layer image.

You will realize that your images are welded when they change to a similar colour and the new image is marked "Welded Image" in the Layers panel.

Edit Panel, Fonts and Images

Lock – Lock the viewpoint proportion so image size changes in extent.

Open – Unlock the viewpoint proportion so you can extend on a flatten designe or vertically without keeping extents the equivalent.

Pivot – Adjust the point of revolution of the chose article.

Mirror Horizontal – Flip a image on a flatten designe.

Mirror Vertical – Flip a image vertically. Flatten Position – Position a image evenly from the upper left corner of the configuration screen to the upper left corner of the image jumping box.

Vertical Position – Position a image vertically from the upper left corner of the design screen to the upper left corner of the image jumping box.

Font style Filter Menu – Filter the font styles by class to change which text styles show up in the font style type menu.

- All Fonts – Display all text styles accessible for use.

- System Fonts – Display text styles found on your PC.

- Cricut® Fonts – Display text styles from the Cricut® library.

- Single Layer Fonts – Display text styles that just contain one layer.

- Writing Style Fonts – Display font styles explicitly intended to be writed with a pen. While most font styles will follow the outside of the letters, writing style font styles include letters with single strokes to make them like transcribed text.

Text style Type Menu – Displays font styles dependent on the picked font filters. Look through font styles for various decisions; selecta font style to apply to the chose text.

Text Style – Choose the font style, normal, striking, italic, strong italic and (when accessible) writing style. Framework text style styles may vary from Cricut font style styles.

- Adjust Left – Align message along the left half of the text box.
- Adjust Center – Align message in the focal point of the text box.
- Adjust Right – Align message along the correct side of the text box.

Layers Panel

Seclude Letters – Ungroup letters in a book box so each letter assembled with its layers appears in the Layers panel as a image. You would now be able to move and resize each letter autonomously, keeping each letter's layers grouped.

Circulate Letters to Layers – Ungroup multi-layered text with the goal that each layer bunch appears in the Layers panel as a image.

Letters will stay assembled permitting you to edit each layer autonomously. Text will be convert to a image.

Letter Spacing – Adjust the space of each letter inside a text box.

Line Spacing – Adjust the space between each line inside a text box.

Cut – Split two covering layers into discrete parts.

Weld – Join numerous layers together to make one shape, evacuating any covering cut lines.

Connect – Hold your cuts in position with the goal that images on the cutting mat will show up precisely as they appear on the design screen. Attach can likewise secure an attract or score layer to a slice layer to tell the machine on which image layer text or score line ought to be put.

Confine – Separate attached layers so they are never again associated and will cut or draw autonomously from every single other layer.

Smooth – Turn any image into a printable image, consolidating every chosen layer into a solitary layer.

Unflatten – Separate layers from a solitary printable image into individual printable layers.

Contour– Hide or unhide shape lines or cut ways on a layer.

- Cut – Set the layer to cut.
- Write – Set the layer to write.
- Score – Set the layer to score.

Print – Turn a layer into a printable image which will be imprinted on a printer and afterward cut on the Cricut® machine. Use flatten to make the whole image print as an item.

Shrouded Layer – Layer is escaped review on the structure screen. Click to unhide layer. Shrouded layers won't cut, print, write, or score.

Unmistakable layer – Layer is noticeable on the structure screen.

Group – Group numerous layers, images, or text together so they move and size together while working with them on the structure screen (won't influence how images are spread out on the cutting mats).

Ungroup – Ungroup a lot of layers, images, or text so they move and size freely from each other on the design screen (won't influence how images are spread out on the cutting mats). Ungrouping text permits you to move and resize each layer of text freely, however keeps the letters assembled.

Copy – Copy and glue a image in one stage to make products of a similar image.

Delete – Remove chosen thing from the structure screen.

Match up Panel

Consolidate colour of a task so as to decrease the quantity of various materials you intend to utilize. Synchronize by hauling a image layer and dropping it on another layer whose colour you need to coordinate.

Canvas Panel

Canvas Panel – Refine the project canvas to coordinate the last undertaking. Edit type, size, and colour to change reviews on the structure screen.

Type – Set a canvas from one of the many canvas classes, and afterward refine the canvas type to coordinate your task so as you make you can likewise image the last structure.

Size – Adjust the stature and width of the canvas to coordinate the tallness and width of the last task. You can browse preloaded measures or redo.

Colour – Choose a colour for the canvas that most intently speaks to the project's colour.

Chapter Four: Apparatus

There are no more cartridges; everything is done carefully with the goal that you can utilize any font style or shape that is on your PC. Furthermore, a large portion of the Cricut machines work over wifi or bluetooth, so you can design from your iPhone or iPad, just as from your PC! The Cricut machines are anything but difficult to utilize, absolutely flexible, and just restricted by your own imagination!

The Cricut Explore Air is a die cutting machine (otherwise known as specialty plotter or cutting machine). You can consider it like a printer; you make a image or structure on your PC and afterward send it to the machine. Then again, actually as opposed to printing your structure, the Cricut machine removes it of whatever material you need! The Cricut Explore Air can cut paper, vinyl, texture, create froth, sticker paper, fake calfskin, and that's only the tip of the iceberg!

Indeed, if you need to utilize a Cricut like a printer, it can do that as well! There is an extra space in the machine and you can stack a marker in there and afterward have the Cricut "draw" your structure for you. It's ideal for getting an exquisite manually written look if your penmanship isn't too incredible.

The Explore arrangement of Cricut machines permits you to get to a tremendous advanced library of "cartridges" rather than utilizing physical cartridges. This implies you can utilize Cricut Design Space (their online structure programming) to take any text or shape from the library and send it to your Cricut to be removed. You can even transfer your own designs if you need!

The Cricut Explore Air can slice materials up to 12" wide and has a little cutting edge mounted inside the machine. At the point when you're prepared to remove something, you load the material onto a clingy mat and load the mat into the machine. The mat holds the material set up while the Cricut sharp edge disregards the material and cuts it. At the point when it completes, you empty the mat from the machine, strip your task off the clingy mat, and you're all set!

With a Cricut machine, the conceivable outcomes are unfathomable! All you need is a Cricut machine, Design Space, something to cut, and your own innovativeness!

What Can I Do With A Cricut Machine?

There are TONS of things you can do with a Cricut machine! It is highly unlikely I could even list every one of the potential outcomes, however here are a couple of well known kinds of tasks to give you a thought of what the machine can do.

Cut out enjoyment shapes and letters for scrapbooking

Make custom, carefully assembled cards for any exceptional event (here's a model)

Structure an onesie or a shirt (here's a model)

Make a cowhide armlet

Make buntings and other gathering beautifications

Make your own stencils for painting (here's a model)

Make a vinyl sticker for your vehicle window

Name stuff in your wash room, or in a den

Make monogram pads

Make your own Christmas trimmings (here's a model)

Address an envelope

Enrich a mug, cup, or tumbler (here's a model)

Engraving glass at home (here's a model)

Make your own divider decals

Make a painted wooden sign

Make your own window sticks

Cut appliqués or blanket squares

Make decals for a stand blender

… and huge amounts of different undertakings that are too various to even think about listing!

Chapter Five: Working With Multiple Lines of text

Utilize the Text Edit panel to make changes to text. From the Text Edit panel, you can pick a font style, text style, and size. You can likewise alter the text arrangement, transcontourthe text into image layers, change the space between letters or lines of text, adjust the size of the text, turn it, and change its position.

Font filter menu – Filter the font styles by classification to change which font styles show up in Font Type menu.

• All Fonts – Display all font styles accessible for use.

• System Fonts – Display font styles found on your PC.

• Cricut® Fonts – Display font styles from the Cricut® library.

• Single Layer Fonts – Display font styles that just have one layer.

• Writing Style Fonts – Display font styles explicitly intended to be written with a pen. While most font styles will follow the outside of the letters, writing style text styles include letters with single strokes to make them like manually written text.

Text style Type Menu – Displays font styles dependent on the picked text style channels. Look through font styles for various decisions; selecta text style to apply to the chose text.

Text Edit Panel

Text Style – Choose the font style, customary, intense, italic, striking italic, and (when accessible) writing style. Framework text style styles may contrast from Cricut font style styles.

Adjust Left – Align message along the left half of the text box.

Adjust Center – Align message in the focal point of the text box.

Adjust Right – Align message along the correct side of the text box.

Disseminate Letters to Layers – Ungroup multi - layered text with the goal that each layer bunch appears in the layers panel as a image. Letters will stay grouped permitting you to alter each layer autonomously. Text will be converted to a image.

Disconnect Letters – Ungroup letters in a book box so each letter grouped with its layers appears in the Layers panel as a image. You would now be able to move and resize each letter freely, keeping each letter's layers assembled.

Letter Spacing – Adjust the space of each letter inside a text box.

Line Spacing – Adjust the space between each line inside a text box.

Ungroup – Align message along the correct side of the text box.

Sync panel

Utilize the Sync panel to unite colour of a task so as to diminish the quantity of various materials you intend to utilize. You can adjust layer hues by hauling a image layer and dropping it on another layer whose colour you need to coordinate.

Model

Before adjusting colour, "Toys" is darker and the train shadow is dark.

Change the colour of "Toys" by hauling the "T," the principal letter of the text, by the dark train in the Sync panel.

Match up panel

"Toys" matches up with the train's shadowing colour and both are presently dark.

Tip: You can drag singular symbols between hues or pick a whole line by hauling the little colour bar alongside the symbols to another colour column.

Canvas panel

Utilize a task canvas on the structure screen to assist you with imagining your last project. The Canvas panel causes you refine an undertaking canvas and change its sort, size, and colour to coordinate those of your project.

Tip: The task canvas is a visual portrayal of your project and won't cut. To choose the canvas, click "Set Canvas" on the left half of the design screen.

Type – Set a canvas from one of the many canvas classes, and afterward refine the canvas type to coordinate your project so as you make, you can likewise imagine the last structure.

Size – Adjust the tallness and width of the task canvas to coordinate the stature and width of the last undertaking. You can browse preloaded estimates or alter it.

Colour – Choose a colour for the undertaking canvas that most intently speaks to the project's colour.

Welding Text

The Weld apparatus joins different shapes to make a solitary tweaked image, expelling any covering cut lines. This can be an incredible method to interface the letters of a word for simple get together.

There are two different ways to weld message together to make a solitary word.

1. Decreasing letter dividing to make letters cover

2. Moving individual letters to cover

Choice 1: Decrease letter dispersing to weld text

Stage 1 Add your text to the design screen and choose the text layer(s) so the bouncing box shows up.

Stage 2 Selectthe Edit tab to review the Edit panel.

Stage 3 Use the Letter Spacing device to diminish the space between letters. Enter a particular number in the Letter Spacing field or click the down bolt to diminish dividing by 1pt additions. Keep on diminishing the dividing until the letters are covering.

Tip: If you are working with multi-layered images, shroud any layers you don't need remembered for the last welded image. The shrouded layers will vanish once the text is welded together.

Stage 4 Click the Layers tab to review the Layers panel.

Stage 5 Click "Weld" in the Layers panel to consolidate the images.

You will realize that your text is welded when it changes over to a solitary layer image and the new image is marked "Welded Image" in the Layers panel. Any place cut ways have met, just the outside cut way remains.

Alternative 2: Move singular letters to weld text

Stage 1 Add your text to the structure screen, and the selectthe text box with the goal that the bouncing box shows up.

Stage 2 SelectEdit tab to review the Edit panel.

Stage 3 Click the Separate Letters button in the Edit panel to separate the text into singular letters.

The letters are changed over into images and can be moved separately. The transformation from a book box to singular images will be mirrored in the Layers panel.

Tip: If you are working with multi-layered images, shroud any layers you don't need remembered for the last welded image. The concealed layers will vanish once the text is welded together.

Stage 4 Arrange the letters so they cover.

Stage 5 Click "Weld" in the Layers panel to consolidate the images.

You will realize that your text is welded when it changes over to a solitary layer image and the new image is marked "Welded Image" in the Layers panel. Any place cut ways have met, just the outside cut way remains.

Attaching to hold cut arrangement

The Attach instrument has two capacities. Joining holds your cuts in a similar situation on the cutting mat as in configuration screen. Attaching likewise secures a write or score line to a cut layer. Follow these means to utilize the Attach instrument to hold your images in position.

Tip: all in all, projects are cut in paper saver mode, so images are consequently set on the cutting mat as near one another as conceivable to monitor material. Joining holds your cuts in position with the goal that images on the cutting mat are situated precisely as they appear on the design screen.

Stage 1. Add images and text to the canvas and orchestrate as wanted.

Tip: Click the Grid On/Ofl catch to actuate the structure screen matrix for help in situating.

Stage 2. Selectthe images you might want to cut in a particular position. You will need to attach by layer or colour.

Tip: You may wish to attach images with more than one colour. To work with the images you should ungroup preceding attaching. The Attach apparatus will change over every chose layer into a solitary colour that will be cut from a similar mat. When layers have been joined, they would then be able to be assembled with different layers without affecting the manner in which the undertaking cuts on the mat.

Tip: In request to join, you should choose in any event two layers to connect together. The exemption is single-layer text, which can be joined without another layer chose. Note that attaching changes over text into a image, so you won't have the option to alter the text once it is joined.

Stage 3. Click the Attach button in the Layers panel.

Tip: Once images are connected, if you might want to alter arrangement, images can be separates by clicking "Segregate" in the Layers panel.

Stage 4. You will realize that your images are connected in light of the fact that are marked "Attached Set" in the Layers panel. At the point when you are prepared to start the cutting procedure, click "Go."

Stage 5. The images are appeared on the mat review precisely as you have them organized on your undertaking. Click "Go" and follow the on screen prompts to cut your project.

Attaching to hold write or score position

The Attach highlight can be utilized to secure a write or score line to a cut layer. If there is more than one layer in a project, any write or score lines must be attached to another layer so they will be written or scored on the right mat.

Cricut machines can write or draw on various materials. The sweet wrapper in model 1 has text that is removed, images that are drawn, and message that is written. Anything that is attracted or written should be connected to another layer.

Model 1

Cut text

Drawn image

Writed text

Joining to hold write or score position

Cricut® machines can likewise add score lines to projects. The crate in model 2 contains score lines. Any task that contains a score line must have the score line connected to another layer.

Model 2

If things are not connected, Cricut Design Space will cut in paper saver mode, which means it will naturally put articles individually cutting mat as near one another as conceivable to ration material. Notwithstanding affixing write or score lines to cut layers, attaching likewise holds your cuts in position with the goal that images on the cutting mat are situated precisely as they appear on the design screen.

Follow these means to utilize the Attach apparatus to affix a write or score line to a cut layer.

Attaching to hold write or score situation

Attaching a write or score line to a cut layer

Stage 1 Design your image as wanted.

Tip: If you will connect a write or score line to a multi-layered image, ungroup the multi-layered image first to abstain from joining every one of the layers together. Text containing a write layer shouldn't be ungrouped before attaching.

Stage 2 Selectthe draw, write, or score line and the layer you might want it set on.

Stage 3 Once images have been chosen, click "Connect" on the Layers panel. Your text will be changed over to a image and the text or your score line will be put on the layer it has been connected to.

Attaching to hold write or score position

Stage 4 You will realize that your images are attached in light of the fact that they will show up as an Attached Set on the layers panel. Click "Go" to start the cutting procedure.

Stage 5 The images will show up on the Mat review screen precisely as you have them orchestrated on your task.

Tip: During the cutting procedure, you will be incited to insert your pen or scoring stylus when fundamental.

Contour

The Contour device permits you to conceal a segment of a image layer by evacuating any undesirable cut lines.

Stage 1 You should ungroup a image first if it has different layers. Select the image and afterward click "Ungroup" at the base of the Layers panel.

Stage 2 Select the image layer you might want to alter.

Stage 3 Click "Shape" on the Layers panel.

All images on the design screen will blur, with the exception of the one you have chosen. The blue lines on the image speak to singular cut lines.

Stage 4 Hover over the zone of the slice line you wish to cover up. The line will go to a darker blue.

Stage 5 Click to conceal the cut line. The line will change to a light blue, demonstrating that it will never again appear as a major aspect of the image and won't cut. Repeat with other cut lines, whenever wanted.

Stage 6 When you are done concealing image cut lines, select a clear territory of the design screen. The concealed shapes no long show up as a feature of the image.

Tip: If you wish to show a cut line once more, select the image and click "Shape." You would then be able to click inside the region of the slice line you wish to appear and the contour will return.

Flatten to Print

The Flatten apparatus transforms any image into a solitary layer printable image. The Flatten device finishes two activities on the double: it transforms your images into printable images and consolidations multi-layered images into a solitary layer. This implies the layers will hold their size and position comparative with one another when they are printed and afterward cut.

- Standard image – a image that is intended to cut; may likewise incorporate draw or score lines

- Printable image – a image that is intended to print thencut

Tip: You can likewise transform an individual layer of a image into a printable layer. Selectthe layer thumbnail in the Layers panel to open the Line Type flyout. Click "Print." Unless the whole image is smoothed, these layers will print thencut exclusively instead of as a gathering.

Follow the means beneath to transform a image into a printable image.

Stage 1 Choose a image from the Cricut® Image Library and add it to the structure screen.

Stage 2 If wanted, include an undertaking canvas and alter the image. At the point when you have completed the process of altering it, selectthe image to choose it. Standard images have the line type naturally set to cut, which is demonstrated by the scissors symbol by the layer thumbnail on the Layer panel.

Tip: Add an undertaking canvas by clicking "Set Canvas" in the left menu of the design screen.

Stage 3 Click "Smooth" in the Layers panel.

Tip: If the standard image contains a draw or score line, the Flatten instrument won't be initiated until the layer is changed to a cut line type or covered up.

Stage 4 All layers of the standard image are smoothed into a solitary layer. The Layers panel shows a printer symbol as the line type, demonstrating the image will print then cut. You would then be able to estimate, pivot and move the image as one item. Click "GO" to start the cutting procedure.

Tip: You should make all colour changes before straightening the image. If you might want to choose different hues for your image once it is straightened, you should unflatten the image, roll out the improvements, and afterward smooth it once more.

Stage 5 The image shows up on the mat review with three cut sensor marks encompassing it (various images will have just three cut sensor marks for every printed page). Click "Print and Go" and follow the onscreen prompts to finish your task.

Tip: The Cricut® Image Library incorporates over a thousand printable images. These images are structured with embellishing designs and were designned explicitly for the Print then Cut component. Printable images are added to the structure screen as straightened images. If they have numerous layers, you can separate the layers by clicking "Unflatten" in the Layers panel.

Print then Cut Overview

Carry a universe of colour to your undertaking with the Print thenCut component. Print your images on your home printer and afterward watch your Cricut Explore® cut them out with high accuracy—no scissors required!

Printable image types

There are two sorts of images you can print then cut: standard images and printable images.

1. Standard images are structured with strong hues. If a standard image has numerous layers, the various layers of the image are indicated separately in the Layers panel. Each layer has a scissor, pen nib, or scoring apparatus symbol as the line type, demonstrating each layer will cut, write, or score.

2. Printable images are structured with ornamental examples. They go onto the design screen prepared to print then cut. They appear in the Layers panel as a solitary layer and have a printer symbol as the line type, demonstrating the image will be imprinted on your home printer then cut on the Cricut Explore® machine.

Tip: You can discover printable images by tapping on the Filters symbol and checking the case stamped "Printables." Select a printable image, add it to your canvas, and afterward click "Go" to print then cut.

Print then Cut Calibration

Utilizing the Flatten apparatus

With the Flatten apparatus, you can transform a standard image into a printable image that you would then be able to remove on your Cricut Explore® machine. The Flatten apparatus not just transforms your image into a printable image, yet additionally straightens it into a solitary layer.

Tip: In request to make any alters to a flattened image, you will initially need to unflatten the image utilizing the device in the Layers panel.

Image filter

Each image is given a reviewp of course. The drain is a little fringe around each image that takes into account increasingly exact cutting. In spite of the fact that we prescribe printing with a reviewp for best cut outcomes, you do have the choice to kill the reviewp on or.

Greatest image sizes for Print then Cut

Each internet browser has various settings for printable territory size, which implies that Print then Cut images have distinctive most extreme sizes relying upon the program you use. If you save a project in one program and later open it another, you may need to alter the image's size as indicated by the program's printable zone settings. The following is a rule for greatest Print then Cut image measures in every program.

- Google Chrome™: 5.5" x 8"

- Firefox®: 6" x 8.5"

- Internet Explorer®: 6" x 8.5"

- Safari®: 6" x 8.5"

Print then Cut across the panel session

The whole procedure, from making the project to the last print then cut, should all be done in the equivalent program and on a similar PC to keep away from mistake. While you can save your Print then Cut task inside Design Space® and return to it, exchanging programs or PCs really busy printing and cutting or sparing a Print then Cut image as a PDF and printing it outside the Design Space® stream will bring about inaccurately measured cut sensor marks. For best outcomes, print then cut your undertaking in a solitary Design Space® session.

Utilizing white materials for Print then Cut

Hued materials or materials containing any sort of example may meddle with the cut sensor marks being b by the Cricut Explore® machine. Utilize 8 ½ x 11" white materials for all your Print thenCut projects. It would be ideal if you utilize the cutting mat suitable for your printable material. We prescribe utilizing the Cricut® LightGrip mat if you utilize standard printer or duplicate paper.

Right position of materials on the cutting mat

Spot your printable material in the upper left corner of your cutting mat legitimately along the upper left edge of the cement on the cutting mat. Be certain the material is straight and contains no wrinkles; this guarantees the machine can appropriately distinguish the cut sensor checks around your image.

The Print then Cut element of Cricut Design Space™ for PC and Mac® permits you to print your images from your home printer and afterward cut them out with high exactness on your Cricut® machine. Print then Cut alignment is a progression of basic cuts, questions, and answers intended to enable your Cricut® to machine cut precisely along the edge of your printed image.

• Cricut Explore Air™ machines are pre-aligned.

• Cricut Explore® machines require alignment if utilizing the Print, thenCut component just because; you will be provoked to adjust when you start the cutting procedure. (If you've printed your project preceding adjustment, put it in a safe spot - you'll have the option to utilize it after alignment is finished.)

If you have to adjust your machine for Print, thenCut, you will be incited to do as such. You can likewise experience the adjustment procedure whenever if you are encountering any errors when removing printed images.

Follow these means to start the procedure yourself: (If you are incited to adjust, start at stage 2.)

Step 1 Once you have marked in with your Cricut ID, select "Alignment" from the Account menu.

Stage 2 Click the Continue catch to start.

Stage 3 Load white 8 ½" x 11" paper into your printer for the adjustment sheet and afterward click the Continue button.

Tip: The Print then Cut component ought to consistently be utilized with white materials. Shaded materials may keep your machine from precisely perusing the cut sensor marks.

Stage 4 In the print discourse box that shows up, watch that the goal is your printer and afterward click "Print."

Tip: The vibe of the print exchange screen may differ based the sort of PC you are utilizing.

Stage 5 Make sure your Cricut® machine is controlled on and associated with your PC. When your machine has been distinguished, place the printed adjustment sheet on the cutting mat as demonstrated on the screen and load it into your Cricut® machine. Turn the Smart Set® dial to the Paper setting and afterward press "Go" on your machine.

Stage 6 Your machine will identify the cut sensor checks around the images and afterward make a test cut around the little focus square. At the point when it is done cutting, DO NOT empty the cutting mat. While the mat is as yet stacked into the machine, investigate the cut lines around the little square in the centre.

• Click "Yes" and afterward "Proceed" if the cut line contacts the printed line right around the little box.

• Click "No" and afterward "Proceed" if the cut line doesn't coordinate with the printed line around the little box. So as to get everything without flaw, you'll stroll through similar advances we secured here.

Stage 7 Your Cricut® machine will make a progression of even and vertical cuts on the adjustment sheet. When your machine is finished cutting, DO NOT empty the cutting mat. Take a gander at the lines on the top and along the correct side of the test print page. Figure out which cuts are fixed or nearest to the print line.

Select the comparing number or letter in the drop-down menus. Click "Proceed" after you have made your determinations.

Stage 8 The machine will cut the bigger square shape. At the point when it is done cutting look at the cut line.

• Click "Yes" and afterward "Proceed" if you are happy with the exactness of the enormous box cut.

• Click "No" and afterward "Proceed" if you feel the cut could be improved. You'll be incited to repeat the procedure to improve the alignment of your machine.

Stage 9 You're finished! Your machine is adjusted; essentially click "Save and Close" to continue.

Changing a standard image into a printable Image

The Cricut® Image Library is brimming with images and font styles that can without much of a stretch be transformed into Print then Cut images. Utilizing the Flatten device makes this simpler than any time in recent memory—simply the click of a catch and you're prepared to print then cut!

Stage 1: Select every one of the layers of the standard image you might want to print then cut.

Changing a standard image into a printable Image

Stage 3: The image currently shows up in the Layers panel as a solitary image and has a printer symbol as the line type, demonstrating that it will print then cut. You will review the dark blueprints of the image on the design screen have vanished, likewise showing it is a printable. Alter your structure as wanted.

Tip: In request to make any alters to your smoothed image, you will initially need to unflatten the image utilizing the device in the Layers panel. This will open the line type flyout, permitting you to change the line type and shade of each layer.

Inserting a printable image

Printable images are structured with enlivening examples and are prepared to print then cut. Simply add them to the design screen and click "Go" to print your images on your home printer and afterward cut them out on your Cricut Explore®.

There are two kinds of printable images:

• Single layer printable images – have one layer, go onto the structure screen prepared to print then slice without being flattened.

• Multi-layer printable images – have different layers, go onto the canvas with various layers previously straightened all together printable image. In any case, you can unflatten the layers to work with every one exclusively.

Follow these means to insert a printable image to the design screen.

Stage 1: You'll locate a wide choice of printable images in the Cricut® Image Library. To find the images, start by clicking "Supplement Image."

Stage 2: Open the Filters menu and check the "Printables" box to search just the images that are particularly arranged for the Print then Cut element.

Tip: A printer symbol found along the base of the image tile additionally recognizes printable images from standard images. This equivalent printer symbol shows up beside the image symbol in the Layers panel demonstrating that the image will print then cut.

Stage 3: Select the image you might want to utilize. The green check in the top corner of the image tile shows that the image has been chosen. The image is added to the plate at the base of the window. You can include more than each image in turn.

Stage 4: Once you've chosen your images, click "Addition Images" in the base right corner.

Stage 5: The images are added to the design screen. You would now be able to move and measure images to envision what they'll look like on your task.

Tip: A printable image shows up in the Layers panel with a printer symbol beside the layer thumbnail, demonstrating that it will print then cut.

Isolating printable image layers

Printable images are straightened and prepared for Print then Cut. Some printable images have different layers that are escaped the structure screen and Layers panel; in any case, you can separate the layers to alter independently or to print then cut them independently. If you unflatten it and unhide any shrouded layers, you can work with the layers separately.

Stage 1: Select a multi-layer printable image from the Cricut® Image Library and click the Insert Image button.

Tip: To effortlessly discover multi-layer printable images, select the Printables and Multi-layer channels from the Filters menu.

Stage 2: At the highest point of the Layers panel, click "Unflatten" to separate the image into layers.

Stage 3: Each printable layer currently shows up as a different layer in the Layers panel. Click "Go" to start the cutting procedure.

Tip: You may need to unhide the extra layers for them to show up on the canvas and print then cut independently.

Stage 4: The images are separated to singular mats dependent on colour and line type. Printable layers, if unhidden, will print then cut as a different images.

Tip: If you don't need every one of the layers of the printable image to print then cut independently, select just those symbols you might want to print as one image and click "Straighten" in the Layers panel. The smoothed layers currently show up as a solitary layer thumbnail in the Layers panel and will print then cut as a solitary image. Every single unmistakable layer that have not been flattened together will print then cut as discrete images.

Change printable layers to a strong colour

Printable images are structured with enhancing surfaces and examples. You can change a printable layer to a strong colour by unflattening the image and altering each layer separately.

Stage 1: Selectthe image to choose it so the jumping box shows up and click "Unflatten" in the Layers panel.

Stage 2: Image layers will be separated in the Layers panel. Image layers may reviewm covered up; assuming this is the case, selectthe crossed out eye to unhide layers.

Stage 3: In the Layers panel, select the layer thumbnail of the printable image. This will open the Line Type flyout.

Stage 4: At the highest point of the Line Type flyout, select "Load up with strong colour." The image will change to dark.

Stage 5: Select another colour for the printable image layer by choosing a fundamental colour, utilizing the custom colour picker, or entering a hex worth.

Tip: Change the image layer back to the first Print then Cut image by deselecting "Load up with strong colour."

Stage 6: Select every one of the layers of the printable image and click "Straighten" to make a solitary image for Print then Cut.

Stage 7: The image shows up in the layer panel as a straightened set. At the point when your project configuration is finished, click "Go" to start the print then cut procedure.

Coordinating Colour with Printable Images

The Print then Cut capacity offers boundless inventiveness. Coordinating the shades of standard images to printable images is simple with the colour palette choices. While coordinating the shades of one standard image to another is done in the Colour Sync panel, when working with both standard and printable images you will utilize the colour palette to pick a proper tint.

Stage 1: Place a standard image and a printable image on your design canvas.

Stage 2: In the Layers panel, selecta layer thumbnail of the standard image to uncover the Line Type flyout.

Stage 3: Choose a tint from Basic Colours that is like the printable image colour you are attempting to coordinate.

Stage 4: Use the custom colour picker to additionally alter the colour by clicking a tint that matches that of your printable image.

Tip: Be certain to coordinate shades of all layers of a standard image before transforming it to a print image. When a standard image has been straightened, the colour can't be changed while in a flattened state.

Consolidating standard and printable images to print then cut together

Every single standard image can be changed to printable images by straightening them or changing the line type to print. You can likewise consolidate standard images and printable images to make a solitary print image.

Stage 1: Select both the standard image and the printable image you might want to join.

Stage 2: Click "Straighten" at the highest point of the Layers panel to consolidate them into a solitary printable layer.

Stage 3: The joined images currently show up in the Layers panel with a solitary layer thumbnail that has a printer symbol beside it, demonstrating that the consolidated images will print thencut as a solitary image. Click "Go" to start the cutting procedure.

Finishing your Print then Cut undertaking

In the wake of finishing your structure on the design screen, you are prepared to click "Go." There are only a couple of extra strides to finish until you're looking as your images print on your home printer and afterward are removed on the Cricut Explore® with high exactness.

Stage 1: When your images are prepared to print thencut, click "Go" on the structure screen.

Stage 2: The printable images show up in the mat review with cut sensor marks set around them. These sensor imprints will be filtered by your Cricut Explore® machine to enable it to figure out where to cut. Click "Print and Go" to start the procedure.

Tip: If you are not marked in, you should do as such to proceed.

Stage 3: The print review screen shows up. Click "Print" and the image with the cut sensor imprints will print on your home printer. (Every PC will fluctuate marginally now, as it will mirror your PC's print settings.)

Tip: Make sure your printer is stacked with white material—paper, printable vinyl, printable texture, and so on.

Stage 4: Place the printed material on your cutting mat as demonstrated in the cut review. Load your mat into your Cricut Explore machine and watch as your image is cut with exactness—it resembles enchantment!

Image filter

Each printable image is given a reviewp as a matter of course. The drain is a little fringe around each image that takes into account progressively exact cutting. Even though we prescribe leaving it on for best cut outcomes, you have the alternative to kill the reviewp on or once you've arrived at the mat review.

Stage 1: Click "Progressively Mat Settings" in the upper left corner of the mat review.

Stage 2: Uncheck the crate to go to the reviewp off. You will review the drain vanish from around the image on the mat review.

Stage 3: Check the case to walk out on/off.

The drain may make the printed image look fluffy or misshaped, however this fringe will be cut off in the cutting procedure, yielding a decisively cut image.

On the mat review Printed with drain The finished edition

Investigating Print then Cut

Why isn't my machine perusing the cut sensor marks?

There are a few factors that can meddle with your Cricut Explore® machine's capacity to search the cut sensor checks accurately so as to print then cut.

1. Lighting

• Direct daylight, overhead understanding lights, or other lighting coordinated toward your Cricut Explore® machine may meddle with the machine's sensors.

2. Material position

• All printable materials must be set in the upper left corner of the cutting mat and applied easily. Off base mat situation or wrinkles in the material may meddle with perusing the cut sensor marks.

3. Cutting mat

- Verify that your Cricut® cutting mat has been set under the mat guides, guaranteeing that the mat is situated cozily against the machines rollers before squeezing the Load/Unload button on the machine.

- For best outcomes, utilize a mat with not many or no imprints or smircesh. A mat with smircesh close to the cut sensor imprints may cause the Cricut Explore® machine to confuse the smears with cut sensor marks.

4. Printable material

- Coloured materials or materials containing any sort of example may meddle with the cut sensor marks being searched by the Cricut Explore® machine. Utilize 8 ½" x 11" white materials for all your Print thenCut undertakings.

- Glossy paper may meddle with the machine's capacity to search the cut sensor marks. We prescribe utilizing matte paper.

- Any smircesh that show up around the cut sensor stamps on your printable material could cause the Cricut Explore® machine to confuse the smears with cut sensor marks.

5. Flotsam and jetsam on the cut sensor light

- Your slice sensor light should be liberated from any garbage. To clean the cut sensor light on your Cricut Explore® machine, clear delicately with a little, dry watercolour paintbrush.

6. Making acclimations to the print settings preceding printing

- Changes made to your printer settings will influence the way your Cricut Explore® machine searchs the cut sensor marks. Make certain to make any acclimations to your printer preceding printing from Cricut Design Space™.

7. Changing programs

- Avoid exchanging internet browsers during project creation and finishing. The whole procedure, from making the undertaking to the last print then cut, should all be done in a similar program to avoid blunder.

- Note: Each internet browser has various settings for printable territory size. If you save an undertaking in one program and, afterwards open it another, you may need to alter the images' size as indicated by the program's printable territory settings.

Investigating Print then Cut

8. Printing to PDF

- Do not save your Print then Cut task as a PDF, as the size of cut sensor imprints will be changed and can make them unintelligible. Print then Cut images ought to be printed and cut in one stream. While you can save your Print then Cut undertaking inside Design Space® and return to it, sparing a Print then Cut image as a PDF and printing it outside the Design Space® stream will bring about inaccurately measured cut sensor marks. For best outcomes, print then cut your undertaking in a solitary Design Space® session.

9. Printer type

- Laser printers use warmth to liquefy the printer toner, though ink stream printers print with ink at room temperature. Cricut® printable materials are good with ink fly printers yet can't be utilized with laser printers, as the warmth could soften them inside the printer and ruin it.

10. Sensor light not driving on

- When the machine is checking for the cut sensor denotes, the sensor light ought to consequently turn on. If for reasons unknown the cut sensor light isn't turning on when the machine is endeavoring to filter the cut sensor marks, take a stab at killing your machine and fueling back on. The carriage should move to and fro and the sensor light should turn on quickly during this time. If the sensor light despite everything doesn't turn on, power the machine off. Push the extra clasp (brace An) and the sharp edge clip (cinch B) into the down situation as though the machine were writing and cutting. If the sensor light turns on, power the machine back on and endeavor the examining procedure once more. If the cut sensor light doesn't turn on when both Clamp An and Clamp B are in the down position and the machine is controlled off, it would be ideal if you contact Customer Care for help.

Including Text

Cricut Design Space™ makes it simple to customize your undertaking utilizing text and various font styles.

Stage 1: Insert text onto the design screen by clicking "Include text," situated on the left half of the structure screen.

A clear book box with a book alter field will show up on the structure screen.

Including Text

Stage 2: Type your text into the text alter field and watch as it show up in the text box. Utilize the "Arrival" key if you need a few lines of text.

Tip: In the Layers panel , the initial barely any letters of the text speak to the name of the gathering . What's more, the principal letter of the text speaks to the individual layers.

Stage 3: Click outside the text alter field to close it. Presently you can move, size, and pivot the text box.

Including Text

Stage 4: To alter your text, select it by tapping the text and afterward click again to with the goal that the text box shows up.

Text jumping box

The jumping box is the container that shows up around your text when it is chosen. Each edge of the jumping box permits you to cause a clickpy to alter.

- Upper left — erase the image
- Upper right — turn the image
- Base left — lock/open the image extents
- Base right — size the image

To review the bouncing box, select the text by tapping on it.

Erase button — Remove the text from the design screen by tapping on the red "X" on the upper left corner of the bouncing box. The text will never again show up on the design screen and will be erased from the Layers Panel.

Text bouncing box

Turn handle — To pivot the text, click and hold the round bolt symbol on the upper right corner of the bouncing box and drag it toward any path. As you make changes, the text revolution will be mirrored in the dim point marker close to the image.

Tip: Image turns on the design screen are for representation just and won't be thought about the mat review except if you join the pivoted image to another layer. If you might want to turn your image for cutting, do as such on the mat review.

Tip: When you hold the Shift key while pivoting your text, it will turn in 45 degree increases.

Text bouncing box

Bolted extents — The shut lock symbol on the base left corner of the jumping box demonstrates you will change the width and tallness at a consistent proportion, keeping the text relative.

Size (bolted extents) — To measure the text with bolted extents, click and hold the resize handle (a blue twofold bolt symbol on the base right corner of the bouncing box) and drag it askew. While you are hauling the resize handle, a size pointer shows up close to the image.

Opened extents — If you wish to open the viewpoint proportion, click the perspective proportion lock. Opening the angle proportion permits you to uninhibitedly resize the image without keeping the width and tallness in extent.

Size (opened extents) — To measure the text with opened extents, click and hold the green compass symbol on the base right corner of the bouncing box and drag toward any path. Hauling the symbol straightforwardly left or right changes just the width. Hauling the symbol here and there to changes just the tallness. You likewise can drag the symbol corner to corner to change that stature and width simultaneously without holding a steady size proportion.

Gathering/Ungrouping Text Overview

Text is added to a book box as a gathering and the groupings fluctuate dependent on the quantity of layers in the font style. A few text styles are single layered. These font styles appear as a solitary layer thumbnail in the Layers panel.

Each letter is grouped with different letters in the text box.

Different text styles are multi-layered. These font styles are assembled twice: layers are grouped and letters inside the text box are assembled. In the Layers panel, each layer of these text styles has as its own layer thumbnail.

Text groups permit you to move, size, and pivot message as a solitary item. If you wish to work with text layers or letters exclusively, you can ungroup them with these instruments:

• Ungroup,

• Distribute Letters to Layers, and

• Separate Letters.

Utilizing any of these devices encourages you make changes to the text by changing over it into a image; be that as it may, the text will never again be editable by writing in the text alter field.

Instruments situated in the Layers panel

Ungroup (multi-layered text) — Separates layers however keeps letters grouped.

Ungroup (single-layered text) — Separates text into singular letters.

Devices situated in the Text Edit panel

Disperse Letters to Layers — Separates layers however keeps letters grouped, just chips away at

multi-layered text

Seclude Letters (multi-layered text) — Separates letters however keeps layers grouped.

Disconnect letters (single-layered text) — Separates text into singular letters.

Isolating letters of single-layer text

Refine the design of your undertaking by isolating the letters of single-layer message so you can work with each letter independently.

Stage 1: Selectthe text to choose it on the design screen.

Stage 2: Click either "Ungroup" on the Layers panel or "Segregate letters" on the Edit panel. When working with single-layer text, the two apparatuses play out a similar capacity. The letters of the gathering are separated and changed over to a image.

Layers panel

Stage 3: Each letter shows up in the Layers panel as a different image. The letters can be moved and altered separately.

Isolating layers of multi-layered text

Refine the structure of your project by isolating the layers of multi-layered text so you can work with each layer independently while keeping the letters assembled.

Stage 1. Select the text to choose it on the structure screen.

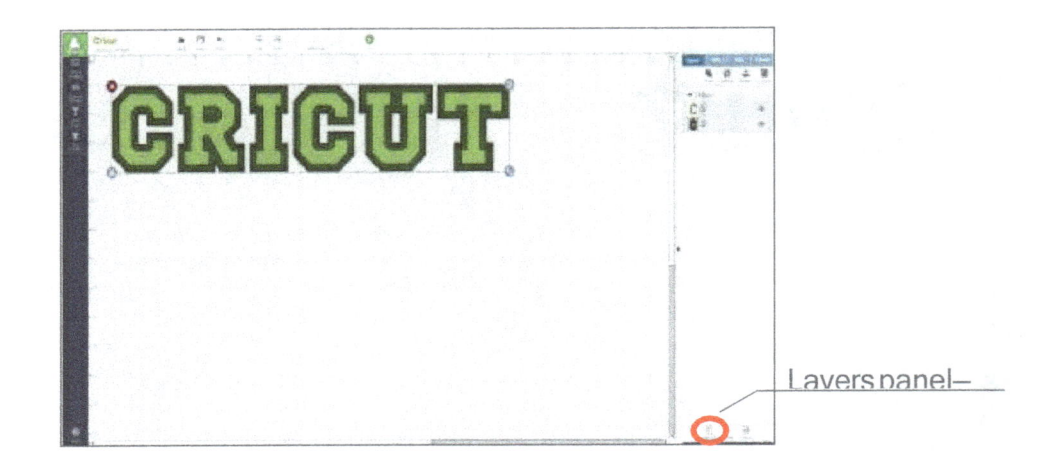

Stage 2. Click either "Ungroup" on the Layers panel or "Disseminate letters to layers" on the alter panel. The two devices for this situation play out a similar capacity. The layers of the gathering are separated and changed over to a image, however the letters of each layer stay assembled.

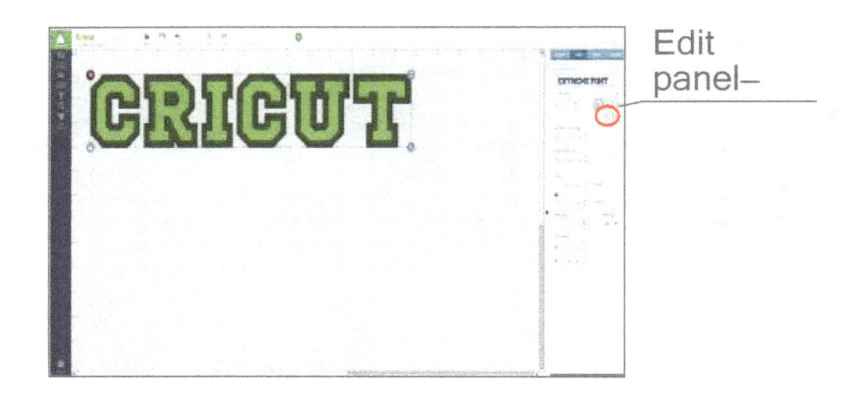

Stage 3. Each layer shows up in the Layers panel as a different image. The layer groups, each with every one of their letters, presently can be moved, estimated, and pivoted separately.

Isolating letters of multi-layered text

Refine the design of your project by isolating the letters of multi-layered text so you can work with each letter separately while keeping the layers grouped.

Stage 1. Select the text to choose it on the design screen.

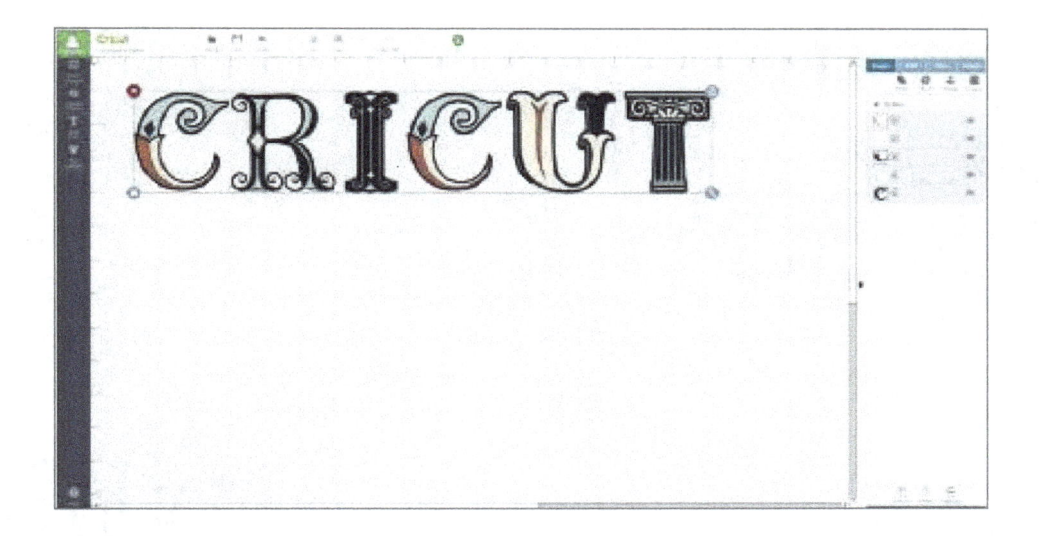

Stage 2. Click "Seclude letters" on the Edit panel. The letters of the gathering are separated, and changed over to a image, yet the layers of each letter will stay assembled.

Stage 3. In the Layers panel, the letters are as yet grouped with their layers. The letters, each with every one of their layers, presently can be moved, estimated, and pivoted exclusively.

Isolating the two letters and layers of multi-layered text

Refine the structure of your undertaking by isolating both the letters and the layers of multi-layered text so you can work with both individual letters and the individual layers of those letters.

Stage 1. Selectthe text to choose it on the structure screen.

Stage 2. Click "Ungroup" on the Layers panel to separate layers. Letters will in any case be grouped.

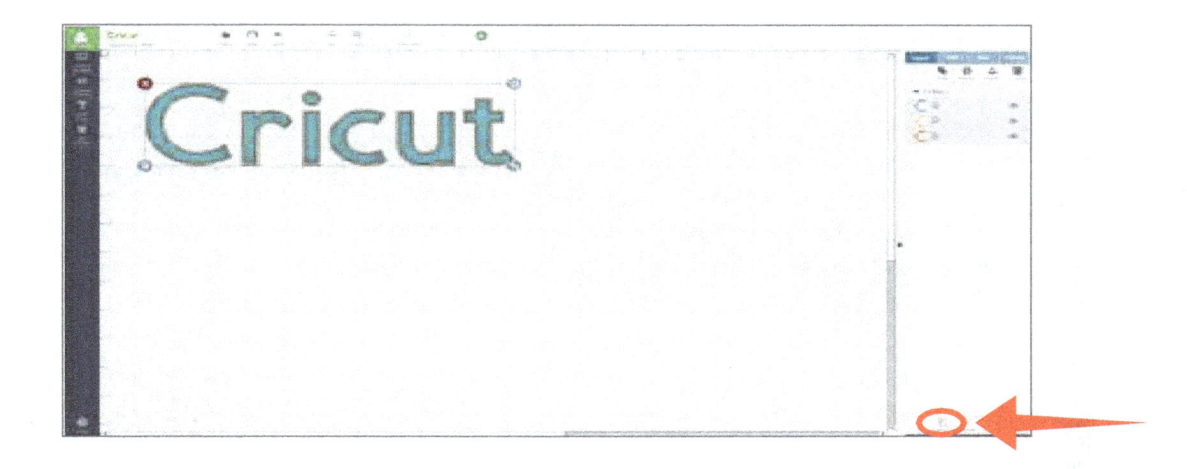

Stage 3. The word is changed over to a image. Each layer presently shows up in the Layers panel as a different image. The layer groups, each with every one of their letters, presently can be moved, measured, and turned separately.

Stage 4. Select a layer gathering and click "Ungroup" on the Layers panel. The letters of the chose layer are separated and each letter is appeared as a different image in the Layers panel.

Stage 5. Repeat the procedure to ungroup the letters of for any outstanding layer groups.

Stage 6. All letters and layers are separated. Each letter and layer of the letter is appeared as a different image in the Layers panel. Letters and layers can be altered exclusively.

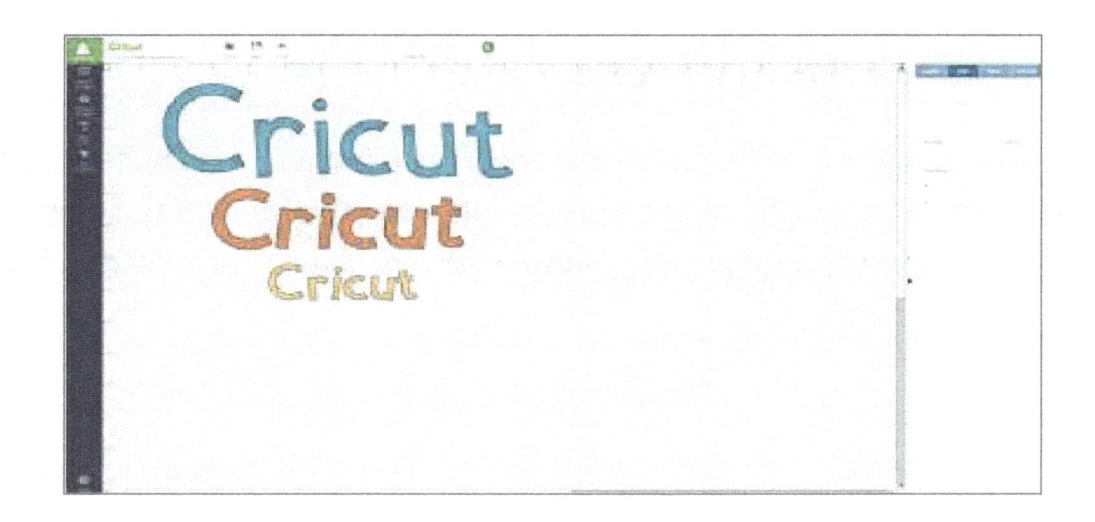

Buying images from the mat review

Structure your task effortlessly utilizing any image in the Cricut Image Library. There is no compelling reason to buy images until you are prepared to begin cutting. Images can be acquired exclusively, in image sets or buy one of the membership intends to approach more than 25,000 images and text styles.

Stage 1 From the mat review screen, you'll review a truck image with the aggregate sum of your buy. Click "Buy".

Stage 2 On the Purchase Summary screen, if you haven't as of now, enter your installment data. When the data has been entered, the spare profile catch will get dynamic. Click "Spare profile" to proceed. (If your installment data has been fileed, you will avoid this progression.)

Tip: Cricut Design Space will spare your data for future buys. You can change your data in the file subtleties screen whenever.

Stage 3 Review your buy list and enter any promotions or limits codes if material.

Stage 4 Enter your secret word in the "Approve Purchase" field, and afterward click "Approve."

Stage 5 Once your buy is finished, you will be come back to the mat review and a message will peruse, "Request was fruitful."

Obtaining images from the Cricut Image Library

Structure your project effortlessly utilizing any image in the Cricut Image Library. There is no compelling reason to buy images until you are prepared to begin cutting. In any case, you are allowed to buy images from the Cricut Image Library whenever. Images can be acquired legitimately from Cricut Design space exclusively, or as a computerized cartridge.

Choice 1 Purchase singular images from the Cricut Image Library

Stage 1 To buy a image, click on "Addition image" from the structure screen.

You will be taken to the Cricut Image Library.

Stage 2 Click on the data symbol on any image tile to show the image subtleties.

Stage 3 Click "Purchase Image."

Stage 4 You will be taken to the Purchase Summary screen, if you haven't as of now, enter your installment data. When the data has been entered, the spare profile catch will get dynamic. Click "Spare profile" to proceed. (If your installment data has been filed, you will avoid this progression.)

Tip: Cricut Design Space will spare your data for future buys. You can change your information in the file subtleties screen whenever.

Stage 5 Review your buy synopsis and enter any promotions or limits codes if appropriate.

Stage 6 Enter your secret key in the "Approve Purchase" field, and afterward click "Approve."

Stage 7 Once your buy is finished, you will get a message which peruses, "Request was fruitful."

Stage 8 Click the "X" in the upper right corner of the shopping window to come back to the Cricut Image Library.

Stage 9 Image will currently appear as obtained in the image tile.

Tip: If the obtained image doesn't appear as acquired in the image tile, sign out of your file and afterward sign in once more. The buy will currently show accurately.

Buying images from the Cricut Image Library

Alternative 2 Purchasing computerized cartridges from the Cricut Image Library

Stage 1 To buy an advanced cartridge from the Cricut Image Library, click on "Supplement image" from the design screen. You will be taken to the Cricut Image Library.

Stage 2 Select the Cartridge file.

Stage 3 Scroll through the various cartridges until you find the computerized cartridge you might want to buy. All computerized cartridge valuing is shown on the correct side of the cartridge tile. You can buy from here by tapping on the "Purchase" choice.

Stage 4 You will be taken to the Purchase Summary screen, if you haven't as of now, enter your installment data. When the data has been entered, the spare profile catch will get dynamic. Click "Spare profile" to proceed. (If your installment data has been fileed, you will skirt this progression.)

Tip: Cricut Design Space will spare your data for future buys. You can change your information in the file subtleties screen whenever.

Stage 5 Review your buy outline and enter any promotions or limits codes if material.

Obtaining images from the Cricut Image Library

Stage 6 Enter your secret phrase in the "Approve Purchase" field, and afterward click "Approve."

Stage 7 Once your buy is finished, you will get a message which peruses, "Request was fruitful." The advanced cartridge will currently appear as acquired.

Tip: If the acquired image doesn't appear as obtained in the image tile, sign out of your file and afterward sign in once more. The buy will currently show effectively.

Access more than 25,000 images and font styles in the Cricut® Image Library with the membership designs. Get a pay-more only as costs arise month to month membership – or a yearly membership for a far superior worth – and utilize a huge number of expertly designnned images and text styles on your activities.

- Monthly membership $9.99 every month

- Yearly membership $99.99 every year

Review a list everything being equal and cartridges remembered for the membership http://text.provocraft.com/b/pdfs/cricutimagelibrarysubscription.pdf .

Tip: Subscription designs can likewise be obtained straightforwardly from Cricut.com. http://us.cricut.com/shopping/items Subscription-257.aspx

Follow these means to add a membership design to any buy.

Stage 1 Review your buy list. Select the arrangement you might want to buy and click "Include this arrangement."

Stage 2 The picked membership design will be added to your buy list and any images that are a piece of the membership will show they are incorporated with the membership buy. Survey your buy list and enter any promotions or limits codes if relevant.

Stage 3 Enter your secret word in the "Approve Purchase" field, and afterward click "Approve."

Stage 4 Once your buy is finished, you will get a message which peruses, "Request was effective."

Stage 5 Click the "X" in the upper right corner of the shopping window to come back to the Cricut Image Library.

Stage 6 Images and cartridges that are incorporated as a component of the membership will currently appear as "Sub-scribed" in the Cricut Image Library.

Tip: If images are not fileed as bought in the image tile, sign out of your file and afterward sign in once more. The bought in images and cartridges will presently show effectively.

Choosing a font style

The alter board in Cricut Design Space works fundamentally the same as the image alter board when estimating, turning and situating text be that as it may, it additionally makes finding the correct font style and altering text basic so you can undoubtedly customize your undertakings.

Tip: You can utilize Cricut font styles just as any framework font style introduced on your PC.

Stage 1: Once message has been added to your project, customize with the ideal font style. Snap on the Edit tab to open the Edit board. There are three font style menus to work with.

• Font Filter menu channels the font styles by classification to change which font styles show up in the Font Type menu.

• Font Type menu shows font styles dependent on the picked font style channels. Look through font styles for various decisions; click on a font style to apply to the chose text.

• Font Style menu offers font style alternatives for normal, striking, italic, strong italic and writing style. (Font style styles alternatives may vary dependent on font style type.)

Tip: Font boxes can just contain one font style anyway you can add the same number of text boxes to a task as wanted.

Stage 2: Click on "All Fonts" to channel for various font style alternatives. There are five choices to browse be that as it may, not all font styles have all choices accessible.

• All Fonts – Display all font styles accessible for use.

• System Fonts – Display font styles found on your PC.

• Cricut® Fonts – Display font styles from the Cricut® library.

• Single Layer Fonts – Display font styles that just have one layer.

• Writing Style Fonts – Display font styles explicitly intended to be written with a pen. While most font styles will follow the outside of the letters, writing style font styles highlight letters with single strokes to make them like manually written text.

Stage 3: The font style name of the chose font style will show up in the Font Type menu. To review extra font style types, click on the present font style name to show the menu. Look through the alternatives or enter a name in the inquiry field and afterward tapping on a font style of decision. The new font style will be shown.

Tip: Use any font style on your undertaking with estimating recorded beside the name for nothing. If you like the look and decide to utilize it on your task, you will be approached to buy the font style preceding cutting.

Stage 4: Fonts frequently have style alternatives. To review extra font style styles, click on the present font style to show the menu. Look over alternatives like: ordinary, striking, italic, strong italic, or writing style (choices differ dependent on the font style picked). When obtaining a font style, all styles accessible accompany the font style.

Tip: Cricut font styles regularly have more than one layer. Turn concealed layers on by tapping on the eye in the layers board. You can conceal layers similarly.

Writing with Fonts

Cricut Design Space offers Cricut font styles explicitly intended to be drawn with a pen and not cut. While most font styles will follow the outside of the letters, writing style font styles include letters with single strokes, so they're the most like written by hand message.

Changing your font style to a writing style

Stage 1: To change your font style to a writing style, select your text and afterward click on the Edit tab to open the Edit board.

Stage 2: Click on the first dropdown in the Edit board to channel for various font style choices. There are five alternatives to look over. Select the "Has Writing Style" alternative to review font styles explicitly structured as drawn with a pen and not cut. Remember that not all font styles have a writing style alternative accessible.

Writing style font styles consequently default to being drawn with a pen as opposed to cut. The text on the design screen will be changed to a Write Line Types.

Stage 3: Choose a font style configuration by tapping on the Font Type menu. Look through the choices or enter a name in the inquiry field and afterward click on a font style of decision. The new font style will be shown.

Stage 4: Click on the Layers tab to open the Layers board. Select the image layer to show the Line Type flyout. Make acclimations to the pen shading.

Tip: You will review the line type is set to write and the shading alternatives have changed to coordinate the shades of the accessible Cricut pens.

Stage 5: You have to show which layer the text ought to be writed on. To do this, you have to utilize the Attach highlight. Ungroup the image you are joining your text to if it has various layers.

Stage 6: Select both the text to be writed and the image or layer you might want it to write on.

Stage 7: Once your images have been chosen, click "Append" on the Layers board. Your text will be changed over to a image and will be written on the layer it has been connected to.

Stage 8: You will realize that your images are joined on the grounds that they will show up as an Attached Set on the layers board. Snap "Go" to start the cutting procedure.

Stage 9: The images will show up on the Mat review screen precisely as you have them orchestrated on your task. Snap "Go" to proceed.

Stage 10: During the cutting procedure, you will be incited to embed your pen when fundamental.

Tip: If things are not joined, Cricut Design Space will cut in paper saver mode, which means it will naturally put items on the cutting mat as near one another as conceivable to preserve material and written text will be put without anyone else cutting mat.

Review your project on the mat review is the last advance before sending your task to the Cricut® machine. On the mat review, you can make some last alters to your undertaking, including:

- Changing project amount,

- Selecting material size,

- Moving images around on the mats, and

- Rotating images on the mats.

For Print at that point Cut projects, you additionally will have the option to choose whether you need the images to print with a reviewp around the edges to guarantee you won't need to trim away any blank area.

To get to the mat review, click "Go" on the design screen.

The entirety of the images on your project will be isolated onto various mats dependent on line type and material shading. Connected images will be set together dependent on choices made on the structure screen.

On the mat review, you can choose the quantity of projects that you might want to make. Snap in the case beside "Project Copies," type in the quantity of duplicates, and afterward click "Apply."

Every one of the images in your task will be copied the same number of times as showed. The images will consequently stream to new mats as fundamental.

You can review every one of your mats by tapping on a mat thumbnail on the rundown at the left half of the screen.

When a mat is chosen, you can roll out a few improvements to it. These incorporate changing the material size, mirroring the images for iron-on material, moving and turning on the mat. Every one of these progressions just influences the mat that is chosen. If you might want to make changes to various mats, you should alter each mat separately.

To change the material size, select an alternative from the Material Size menu. Select an alternate choice. As of now, print at that point slice is constrained to 8.5" x 11" material.

Tip: The Material Size menu just offers material sizes bigger than the biggest image on the mat. As of now, Print at that point Cut mats are constrained to 8.5" x 11" material.

You can turn mirroring on or off by checking the container marked "Mirror (for iron-on)." All the images on the mat will be mirrored (flipped once evenly). Images will reviewm turned around when cut. This is especially significant if you are utilizing iron-on as your material; if you don't mirror the images, they will show up backward when pressed on.

Tip: Mirroring just influences the chose mat. If you wish to mirror more than one mat, turn mirroring on for each mat independently.

Images will consequently be put on your mat as appeared in the mat review. You have the alternative to move images around on the mat review for favored arrangement.

To move images, drag the image to the ideal area. Bouncing boxes can cover; in any case, remember that cut lines that cover on the mat review will cut into each other.

To pivot a image, select it by tapping on it and afterward drag the turn handle to pivot the image in either course. The turn handle is a hover symbol at the top focus of the jumping box; when you click it, a bended bolt shows up.

When you are happy with image situation, click "Go" to continue to the cut screen.

Tip: If you are not marked into your Cricut account, you should sign in with your Cricut ID before proceeding.

Mirroring images for iron-on

When working with iron-on material, you can identical representations on the mat review so they can be effectively applied. Images will reviewm turned around when cut. If you don't mirror the images, they will show up backward when pressed on.

Stage 1: Once you are finished structuring your project, click "Go" in the top menu of the design screen.

Stage 2: Select the mat on which you will utilize iron-on material and check the crate marked "Perfect representation (for iron-on)". Rehash independently for each mat that will cut with iron-on material.

When you select the mirror choice, the images will mirror the change on the mat review.

Tip: If you have set the Smart Set® dial to press on however didn't mirror your images on the mat review, you will get an alarm on the cut screen. If you wish to mirror the images, just come back to mat review, check the Mirror checkbox, and afterward click "Go" to come back to the cut screen.

Load, Set, Go

Stacking the mat into the machine, choosing the material on the Smart Set Dial™ and advising your machine to cut are your last strides in cutting the venture.

Stage 1: Once your task is finished, click "Go" on the top menu of the structure screen to start the cutting procedure.

Tip: We prescribe sparing your undertaking before continuing to the mat review screen. Snap "Spare" on the top menu of the structure screen to put a duplicate of the design in your undertakings.

Stage 2: On the mat review, survey your cutting mats and roll out any ideal improvements. At that point, click "Go" on the base right corner of the mat review. If you haven't just done as such, you should sign in with your Cricut ID and buy the required pictures.

Stage 3: Load your mat into your Cricut® machine keeping mat pushed immovably against rollers, and afterward

Tip: If you are associated by means of Bluetooth and USB, you might be incited to select the best possible association at the highest point of the screen.

Stage 4: Turn the Smart Set dial to the ideal material. If you select "Custom" on the dial, you will likewise need to choose the suitable material starting from the drop menu on the cut screen.

Stage 5: Click the flickering Go catch to start the procedure. On the off chance that important, you will be incited to embed your pen or scoring stylus at the fitting time.

Tip: If an inappropriate material setting was chosen on the dial, press the Pause button on the machine to stop the cut. Turn the dial to the right material setting and press Pause again to keep cutting. When the cuts are finished, if you have to